A
Before
Insanity

Sherese L. Jordan

outskirts
press

Author's note: To protect the privacy of certain individuals the names and some specific places have been changed.

Table of Contents

Acknowledgments vii

Prologue xv

1. A Child's Silent Cry 1

2. Poor Lil' Rich Girl 9

3. 'Til Death Do Us Part...13

4. Suffering The Consequences 21

5. Getting Acquainted to The One Who Conceived Me ...33

6. In Bondage...41

7. Motherless Child...53

8. Existing in Limbo 63

9. Flown From The Cuckoo's Nest.....................................70

10. Green Vision, Brown Reality...80

11. The Tornado Hits The Roof..86

12. An Act of God 96

13. A Pastor is Only Human; He's Not God 98

14. Hustling: Back to The Dirty-Dirty 106

15. Faith's Results 113

16. Sheeps in Wolves Clothing..117

17. Down in the Valley...124

18. 22 Weeks Too Long 136

19. Tainted Love 149

20. Joel 2:28..163

21. The Signs 173

22. The Havoc 176

Epilogue 184

About the Author 186

Acknowledgments

To my Father in heaven, who is the head of my life: I give you ALL the honor, the glory, and the praise. Thank you for giving me the inspiration and burning desire to compose this project. You blessed me to reach out vastly across the world to people who feel hopeless in life and without destiny because of their life's experiences. Thank you for using me to reconstruct and redirect the lost souls in a positive way. Thank you, Father, for using me as a guiding light in the darkest places, leading your children straight to you. Father, please continue to use me in any way you please. I love you and I Do Lift Up The Name Of Jesus. Thank you, God, for Jesus – Thank you, Jesus, for being our bridge to God over troubled waters!

To my faithful & loving husband, Joel J. Jordan, thank you forloving me as much as you love you. Thank you for being the best husband and stepfather. Thank you for standing by my side faithfully through all that I have gone through. God used you to take me out of the 40-year wilderness I lived, literally. Sharing my life with you has enabled me to live outside the box to view inside of what used to be my life; a touch before insanity. God placed you in my life as my earthly guardian angel. #I Love You!

Husbands ought to love their wives as their own body: Ephesians 5:28

To my children: Traevon, Ahkeem, Ahkwaan, Don and (the late) lil' Miss Deva, and stepchildren Tezz wit' two Z's and Marcia. You've loved me unconditionally, understood me, believed in me, and never judged me. You've always respected me and treated me like a queen; I LOVE YOU GUYS!

*To my beautiful queens and mothers of my grandchildren:
Ramada, Anequa, Michelle, and Imani; Women of noble
character, you are God's precious jewels. Thank you for being
an addition to the family and ideal mothers to my beautiful
God-given grandchildren Armani, Mar'Von, Brook'lyn, King,
Ah'Miya, Eve, Canaan, Naomi, Mylah, Maliyah, and Miguel.*

*Thank you, Father, for carrying my grandson King
through his long journey in a severe storm. Thank
you for his strength, because he certainly remained
strong through it all; that's what Kings do!*

*I thank you, Donald, for your many years of being a dedi-
cated father and for opening my eyes; you enlightened me to the
world of womanhood. You taught me how to fly from the nest.
Thank you for loving us unconditionally. I love you dearly!*

*A great appreciation goes out to my dad and step-
mother, James and Lula, for being awesome parents,
grandparents, and great-grandparents. You filled a massive void in my life where my mother didn't understand how to, and for that, I am humbly grateful*

*I thank my father-in-law, the late Pastor John H. Jordan,
founder of Let Them Come MBC in Detroit, MI. You in-
terceded on behalf of my mother before the Lord called
her home; thank you. Thank you for your obedience to
the Father in ordering my steps to stay rooted in the "D,"
I would've walked away from a True God fearing Man
that the Lord designed to be my husband-literally!*

*Pastor Cornell D. Sampson (nephew), Evangelist
Rosa Jordan (cousin), and The late Reverend Angie
Peterson: Thank You all for empowering me, and allowing the Father to use you to build me up where I was
torn down. I am truly grateful for you. I love you!*

Sister Constance Faulk, Thank You, for passing your choir robe onto me, it gave me courage to face a multitude. It was confirmation from the Lord that I am indeed a motivational speaker. I love you!

I love and Thank You dearly Pastor John Manning & first lady Manning.

I thank you, Pastor Terry Caldwell of Rock Church International in Detroit, MI. Thank you for the prophetic messages you spoke to me. You enlightened me along this very long journey. Whenever I came to you with a problem, you didn't pamper me with words, but yet kept it real and straight to the point. I will always love that about you. I removed all dead weight out of my life in the same manner!

Thank You Prophet and Prophetess Allen & Gabrielle Pullins Pullins of Straight Faith Ministries in Southfield MI. You two have such a high anointing on you, and one of the most fervent and powerful spirits given from God; I've never had such a close encounter with the spirit until you two prayed over me. I feel free, after literally living 40 years in the wilderness. Thank You!

Thank you, Aunt Patricia, Godmother Niecy, and Cousin Angel for being attentive to my dreams. You took time out of your precious life to listen to my voice concerning this project. I was expecting to be critiqued, but didn't get that; instead you gave me eminent motivation that enhanced my self-confidence even more.

YOU BELIEVED IN ME!

To the (late) Henry and (late) Ruth: I love and miss you so very much, Grandma and Grandpa. I only have good memories coming up when you were here. My intentions were to accomplish my dreams before you went on to glory, but of course God had his own timing, for which I'm truly grateful. He used me when he was ready, because he knew that you would still be able to be proud of my success, looking down on me from heaven.

Thank you, my baby brother Immanuel (Troub), for your loyalty, and faithfulness. I love you!

Thank you Troub and cuz Monique - aka Mo for being my umbrella during my storm when I laid my daughter to rest; I love you guys. Thank you, Mo, for rockin' her sweatshirt faithfully every year on her birthday.

To my cousin Cindy: Thank you so much for your comfort, encouraging words, and much-needed support. I love you!

I thank my aunts and uncles for loving and supporting me through the years: (the late) Dennis, the late Allen, Debra, Michael, Linda, Kimberly, Bettie, Debbie, Ronnie, and Dennis, aka DJ.

I truly love my cousins, "The Beautiful DIVAS": Naketah, Tracie, Chelsea, Monique, Jacquise, Rochelle, Kelly, Khalia, Kim, and Alaina. I love my cousins "Young Kings": Anthony, Evan, Krasne, Bronson, Jacquoy, and Chance (aka Jeeprs Creeprs) – I Love You, Boy!!!

Cassandra, thank you for being a dedicated and faithful friend of many years. I love you!

To my inlaws; the Jordan family: I thank all of you for genuinely embracing me from day one! A lot of the times those types of relationships are messy. Thank God you all were a blessing to me. I love all of you!

To my baby - mama Areia and Godmother to my children my children. On the reverse side; I love and cherish my beautiful godchildren always: Shinice, Shian, Kayla, and Jason.

I love and give special appreciation to the B-family—Bridget, Britney, Briana, Brandy, and Brandon—for loving my daughter genuinely and supporting me through the aftermath (you will forever be engraved in my heart, Briana).

I love and thank you, Martez, for genuinely being there for our family through the rough times.

Much love to you, Poochie, for your loyalty, honesty, and 100% support to me and my children, and a shoulder to cry on during my greatest trials. (I understood your place and position; I also knew your heart pumped for my children and me for the well-being of our lives.) Poochie, you filled voids in my life where they did not. I thank you from the core of my heart for being obedient to the Father and allowing him to use you where you were most needed in our lives.

I love you, Alvin (aka L.B.)!

Thank you, Aunt Katie, cuz Renee, sister Taul, and sister-in-laws Choya and Ruthie; I love you guys!

Mann (nephew), always remain humble and handsome, and you my niece Kayja the Queen, stay Beautiful and Glowing. I love you two!

I love you, Shirley, Carmela, Marvin, Martez, Destiny, Trina, Shamika, and Phat-Phat.

Lorraine, I thank God for you. You are another one of God's precious jewels…I will always love you!

I love you, Nikki and Carolyn; I will always keep you two tucked down in my heart.

I love you always, Mama Joyce!

I thank the GoFundMe fund-raising service and supporters for helping to make my passion a reality.

Thank You, Outskirts Press publishing. Thank You Cindy for that Beautiful cover design, it looks exactly how I envisioned it.

Thank you, Bishop T.D. Jakes, for your intriguing and uplifting sermons. Your spiritual insight has played beyond an essential role in the woman I've become. I Am a Living Legacy! The sermons from Bishop T.D. Jakes, Joyce Meyers, and Joel Osteen renewed my mind when the devil told me over and over again that God didn't love me and I was a nobody and would never be successful. All three of you were my spiritual medication; you gave me what no doctor in the world could prescribe. Thank you!

Thank you, Rick Warren, for The Purpose Driven Life. You redirected my thinking process and answered questions concerning trials that took place in my life that I had been confused about for years. Dear God, thank you!

I Love You LTC MBC, Rock Church International, you are a Powerful church!

Thank you, Mary Mary, for uplifting my spirits through your music when I was weak and feeble.

The late Great Whitney Houston - Forever my Diva! I love and thank you so very much for inspiring me through my childhood years and into my adulthood. I remember when I started to give up on writing and your song "Miracle" played on the radio; out of all your songs, that was one I hadn't heard since my childhood. I felt you singing to me when suddenly praises to God took over me. I started believing again. I got up, continued writing, and completed it!

Last, but definitely not the least,

I am so grateful for each and every last one of my enemies. Your unfaithfulness, evil desires, stabs in the back, and biting tongues that spat out venom were the root of my strength, my courageousness, and my drawing closer to the Father, which also led to the writing of this book.

I was ordained to reach out to millions across the world who are severely wounded and lost because they feel unloved and like there's no way out…like the way I used to feel. I give my enemies excellent credit; I thank and love all of you genuinely, because you were also an essential part of the woman I've become today. I realize that you are definitely significant in this world, so give yourselves a great big round of applause!!!

The Lord said to my Lord "sit in the place of honor at my right hand until I humble your enemies, making them a footstool under your feet." Psalms 110:1

(Every demon has its place!)

I thank God dearly for each and every one of you that I acknowledged. I am stronger, much wiser, confident, and victorious.

NOW I BELIEVE IN ME!

Thank you, Father in Heaven, for the mother you blessed me with. Thank you, Mother, for loving me in your own special way, because it was better than no love at all. Thank you for giving me life, and leaving me your strength. We need strength in this cold world in order to overcome all of our obstacles. There's no love in money; money can't pay for peace. Strength is priceless and lasts forever; it was the best nourishment you could have ever given me and I am humbly grateful. I love you!

Thank you, Father, for the daughter you blessed me with for seven beautiful years. Deva, now I understand why you wanted to spend every moment of your life with me; you were only here for a short while. Now I understand. Seven has always been my favorite number because spiritually it represents completion. Everything happened just the way it was supposed to happen; it was God's Will. God blessed the seventh day and made it holy, because on it he rested from all the work of creating that he had done; Gen. 2:3.

Part 1

Prologue

Lying in bed, a quarter to midnight, I can hear the sounds of footsteps as they near my room. I know what time it is. It's a nightly ritual. How I found myself in this situation, the memory is vague. As my door creeps open, I get myself prepared for what I am about to do.

Darren Jr. walks into my room and sits on the edge of my bed. Everyone is sleeping as usual. I am only five years old. I don't know what I am doing, all I know is that it has to be done in secrecy and that it feels wrong.

Who would have known this would be the start of a chaotic life full of abuse, love, lies, hurt, and deceit. This was the start of my touch before insanity.

1

A Child's Silent Cry

Detroit city. Born and raised an only child. Shinice is my name. Diane, my mother, was born in Brooklyn, New York. Diane was a mail carrier for the U.S. Postal Service. She was a hardworking, hustling woman. When push came to shove, she did what she had to do to survive, be it good or bad. Diane was an undercover thug with class. Never cross her...she was definitely gonna get you back by any means necessary.

My dad, Jalin, was from Detroit. He, too, was a very hard worker and full of ambition. He worked for Ford Motor Company, but was drafted into the U.S. Army. After serving his country and receiving an honorable discharge, he later started working with children as a substitute teacher.

My grandparents had seven children and Diane was the one who had to babysit them all while both my grandparents worked; this resulted in her making a vow to herself to have one child only.

As an infant I had a habit of bouncing my head on the bed, wall, or floor. I picked the habit up after Diane was shot in the arm right in front of me, because of God knows what. I assume the sound of the gun triggered my nerves and traumatized me; banging my head was more than likely my comfort.

My parents separated when I was very young. Diane was caught sleeping with some guy named Darren. As her way of dealing with her guilt and repulsion about the affair, she went after my dad with an iron. My dad, raised to be a God-fearing man, continued to be a Father to me, but walked away from the relationship peacefully, and he never looked back.

Diane and Darren continued their relationship and decided to move in together. Darren was a nurse with three sons who lived in Ohio. Every year Darren Jr., Kevin, and Mark came down for summer vacation. Darren Jr. and Kevin had the same mother, and Mark was their stepbrother. Of course there was baby mama drama between Diane and the boys' mothers, I know for sure with Mark's mother. I remember sitting in the car with them one day. Diane and Darren and I were parked in front of Mark's house, and his mother ran up and bricked the front windshield while I was in the car; I was only three at the time. Can you imagine how frantic I was? From that moment everything went blank; it's likely that I became even more traumatized.

Darren Jr. was thirteen, Kevin was eleven, and Mark was seven. As vague as I can remember, the four of us got along okay other than Darren Jr. and Kevin scaring me every time a thunderstorm hit. It was their way of manipulating me into doing what they told me to do, or the thunderman would come for me; typical tactics that older siblings used to stay in control of the youngest.

Every night after everyone went off to bed, I found myself giving Darren Jr. oral sex. I didn't know what a penis was or what I was doing. I only knew something about it wasn't right, because it was done in secrecy. I can't remember if he threatened me about the thunderman or not, but I know something caused me to do such a horrific thing. I can't say I was raised around such, as to where I ever saw or caught Diane and Darren in the act. I don't know where the idea came from besides Darren Jr. maybe manipulating me into it, considering he was thirteen and I was only five. I didn't know how to tell Diane, because I didn't understand it myself. Plus, I didn't want to cause any more family problems than we already had, so I kept it bottled up inside.

Diane and Darren were only good for five things: drawing blood from each other from fighting, drinking, smoking weed and partying a lot and then back to fighting some more. She was doing all of the above before she was pregnant with me, during her pregnancy with me and after I was born. So many times I thought about escaping the madness; I wanted to just run outside and dodge across Grand River straight into ongoing traffic. However, I feared that just as much as I feared telling Diane what I was doing every night.

Every morning Diane dropped me off at my grandparents' on her way to work. My grandmother's friend had a daughter named Latoya, whom I looked up to because she was five years older than I. One day her mother was on the phone while she and I were in her room, and she was telling me about a game called "The Kitty Teaser." The object of the game was to lick each other's vagina. She suggested that I go first, and there I sat, looking gullible and full of bewilderment. Perplexed about the situation that was already going on in my very own home every night; it was the same thing, just with a girl. Yeah, I did it, again not knowing why; I just know licking her kitty made me feel even guiltier than giving oral sex to Darren Jr. I wasn't used to seeing same-sex relationships.

Later that evening I told Diane, but still didn't spill the beans about me and Darren. No legal action was taken, but as far as street action, you couldn't put anything past Diane. I only remember that I wasn't allowed to be around that girl anymore. And telling my dad never even registered in my brain as far as I can remember.

Two years later Darren and Diane bought a beautiful house on the east side. Diane asked her friend Sheryl to babysit me since she lived much closer versus commuting back and forth to my grandparents'. Each morning Diane dropped me off at 5:30 and I'd lie next to Sheryl until sunrise and the other children she babysat arrived. Sheryl had an eighteen-year-old brother named Craig. Every morning he came to Sheryl's bedroom door after she fell back asleep and whisper for me to come to him. I tried pretending I was asleep too, but I knew he knew I wasn't. I kept my eyes closed for almost ten minutes and when I opened them he was still standing in the doorway watching me with a sinister look in his eyes. I was extremely frightened, so as usual I got up and followed him to his room. I was being raped by Craig again and again, repeatedly every day sometimes twice. He said if I ever told Diane he would kill us both, so I didn't tell a soul because I believed him and I was so fearful of him, especially me being seven years old and him eighteen, weighing every bit of 250 pounds. I'll never forget this one time when he pounded my vagina so hard, blood dripped like a heavily leaking faucet.

I went home day after day holding in more secrets. Every day I was being sexually molested at Sheryl's house to going home at night giving Darren Jr oral sex.

Why me? I couldn't understand what was actually going on in my head or my life; just looking at the pattern of things, I thought it was something I did. Why did everybody want to rape me? I felt like the only child this was happening to and it made me feel weird, different, and alone. I would hear whispers saying, "You have to tell," but I didn't have the courage. I was overwhelmed by fear.

On some occasions Diane picked me up early from Sheryl's and let me hang out at the bar with her to kill time before she clocked out from work. She was a fast and accurate worker, so every day she had to stall time for two hours, because you had to clock out at the designated time. So Diane would hang out at the bar with some of the people she delivered mail to on her route and shoot pool. I played the pinball machine and even shot pool sometimes. I didn't know if children were allowed in bars and I didn't care. I was just so grateful to hang out there instead of lying on my back getting raped throughout the day and dealing with just about the same thing at home.

Lying in my bed one night I found myself praying to God and blowing kisses to the angels until my lips were tired. Praying was the one thing I didn't think to do when I was getting sexually abused, because I didn't know how to pray for help. I attended a Catholic Academy, but I don't remember being taught how to pray for help. All I remember from attending that school was Jesus being born to Mary. Probably going to church with my dad on some weekends had an influence on me or maybe God introduced himself. I only knew how to say good-night prayers and blow kisses to the angels, that's it.

Darren and Diane decided to get married after shacking up for eight years. They were married at home in front of the fireplace and I was the flower girl. The reception took place there as well. I loved the new neighborhood. It was beautiful, predominantly white; there were only two black families on the block other than us.

I guess to a degree there was a benefit to them getting

married, because Darren was always the first one home from work which meant I no longer needed Sheryl to babysit me anymore. I enjoyed playing with my new friends; I was just self-conscious because I didn't feel normal like all the other kids. I felt different, the only child experiencing this type of trauma; I felt immortal. Darren always took his sons and me to Kmart. He loved fishing and had a fish tank, so he bought everything he needed for the tank, even new fish. He also bought the boys anything of their choice, but not me. I couldn't even get a candy bar. At first I didn't understand, until it hit me that I wasn't his biological child.

I was standing in the front yard watching my friends play across the street. I was listening to the Emotions' "You Got the Best of My Love" vibrating from the front door. I was reluctant to go across the street to play with the other kids. I felt the entire world knew everything about my life, and each time I stepped foot outside my home, I thought everybody was watching and whispering. My self-esteem was below zero. I would cry inside, hoping that would help and make it go away, but instead it got more intense.

"You have to tell your mother." That whispering voice kept repeating itself, but now the whispers had gotten even louder and those words echoed in my ears over and over and over again. Still, I didn't want to tell Diane because of the enormous fear I felt and also the extreme shame. My brain felt as if it was about to explode. I couldn't take it anymore, so I finally cried out to Diane.

Diane took me to the doctor, but they were unable to detect anything because over a year had gone by. We stopped by Sheryl's house straight from the hospital and Diane told her everything. Sheryl was devastated; she was still coping with the death of their mother, who had recently passed, and now to learn that her brother was a pedophile nearly put her over the edge. She said, "I had no idea." She was sincerely apologetic. I mean, what else was to be expected from her? It wasn't her fault. Diane pressed charges against Craig and every time we attended the hearing, he sat three rows behind, looking directly at me with looks to kill. I was petrified. When it was all over, he was never charged. The court dropped the case because too much time had passed before I cried out for help. However, as fate would have it, Craig ended up murdered.

As far as Darren Jr., Diane never pressed charges against him, I guess because of her love for Darren. It was only agreed that Darren Jr. was never allowed to spend summer vacations with us again, but even that was argumentative. Darren's other sons never came back to visit either. Now all I had to do was continue to deal with Darren and Diane's usual fighting and drawing blood. Most importantly, I had to cope with me and all I had gone through, because I never had counseling. What a confused and traumatized child I was!

I had company over one weekend and Darren and Diane ended up having their usual fistfight—how embarrassing. To retaliate, Diane poured bleach in Darren's fish tank and it resulted in him blacking out. Enraged, Darren snatched my puppy out of my arms, raised him up to the ceiling & body-slammed him to the floor with full force. I watched my puppy lie there in excruciating pain, unable to cry, crippled and folded up like a chicken wing on the floor with broken bones. I went into shock. Life skipped to me only remembering Diane divorcing Darren and him moving out crying, because he didn't want to end the marriage.

Back to what I called a normal life, something I felt I didn't have much of, because my self-esteem hadn't matured at all; it'd only gotten worse. I still felt different from any other kid, as if I didn't fit into the world. I couldn't tell a soul what was going on in my life. I thought I was the only child who was traumatized and lived an unstable life, and I was afraid of being teased. I never told my daddy anything, because Diane trained me not to tell him or anybody else anything. She knew my dad would've filed for custody, and she wasn't having that. Plus, I was never around him after he rightfully whooped me with a switch once for pulling a knife out on a girl up the block. Diane was pissed at him and manipulated me into being mad and not wanting to spend time with him anymore. She just wanted to ban him from me because of her own guilt. She probably didn't want to feel embarrassed or look stupid in front of him because of her and Darren's failing relationship and that pedophile stepbrother of mines.

> *It is because of your value in your soul that you have been attacked in your flesh.*
> *Bishop T.D. Jakes*

2

Poor Lil' Rich Girl

Other than Ladondra, Nina was another one of my best friends. I met both of them in elementary. I met Ladondra first; she lived in the same neighborhood as Sheryl and Craig did, and I attended the elementary school around there. When everything went down with Craig, Diane changed my school of course and that's when I met Nina and Crystal. Nina lived across the street from me, she was the oldest of seven siblings. She had natural long, thick black hair, baseball-bat legs, and Dolly Parton breasts. I was eight years old when I met her at the neighborhood park. I had a pack of Hostess chocolate cupcakes and gave her one, and from there on we became the best of friends.

Crystal lived down the street, and she had the largest donkey-booty I'd ever seen on a child at our young age. Lil' girls looked like lil' girls back in the '70s and so did Crystal, but she had the butt of a mature thirty-year-old woman. Crystal came from a large family of mostly men, so when she fought a woman, it was like fighting a feather, one blow straight in the wind; she was another Diane. Me, I was always known as the prettiest one according to them; a light brown sugar skin tone, tall, skinny, fair length of hair, and just as crazy as I wanted to be. Nina had the boobies, Crystal had the booty, and I had the beauty.

Attending middle school was one of my best memories. Everyone in the class stuck together like glue; back then it was class against class. The girls fought with other classroom female students, but most of our battle was through basketball. We took our animosity out on the courts, and whoever lost lost, and whoever won won…period. Of course we got physical from time to time like the average middle school kid, but we weren't killing each other.

I was the giving one, the one who kept bags full of penny candy, making sure I had enough for all my girls. I even bought each of them their favorite record; the single hits they used to make on 45s. I don't know why I was so giving and friendly, maybe because I was an only child. I had so much love in my heart, and giving to others was my passion. There was one girl named Trina; she used to call me poor lil' rich girl, but I didn't pay any attention to her. I still treated her like I treated the others. I can't help that I was the only child and lived in a beautiful home, and Diane bought me everything. When all said and done, I was still a traumatized, sexually abused child. Poor lil' rich girl fitted my life's description to a tee. Little did Trina know it all came with a price; she had no idea how unstable my life was.

Derf was my middle school sweetheart—hardly my taste in a young man, but heck, we've all dated someone at one time or another and wondered, *What the heck was I thinking?* We only dated for part of the school year, but we remained close friends. He came by to visit me and Diane every day.

I started working part time at a hardware store, making minimum wage. Every payday Diane took me to cash my check and I gave her half, just on the strength of my love for her and the fact of her being my mother. Once the summer job was over and the school semester started, I thought she would do the usual and buy all my clothing, but she didn't. When I approached her about it, she said, "You had a job and you knew you needed things for the upcoming school year, so you should have bought what you needed."

"Mom, I split half of my check with you!"

She told me that was something I chose to do; all she wanted was gas money. Funny how she didn't reject my money when I offered it. I only worked the part-time job for two months, and was paid biweekly. I made just enough to buy underwear and personal hygienic products and I held on to the rest to carry me to the next pay period. I couldn't understand why Diane did that to me. She could afford to buy me nice clothes, which she always did, but not this time. Thank God for my aunt Lynn being a model; she started giving me all her clothes and matching shoes. I was known for dressing like a lady.

I attended Denby High School when I wanted to. On top of being self-conscious and having low self-esteem, I was ashamed of not having anything decent to wear once school started. The new Top 10's had just come out in the shoe stores. They were close to a hundred dollars, and I begged Diane for a pair. She made it clear that if she bought them, they would be the only pair I was getting for the school year, but I didn't believe her. I was her only child and I knew she would buy me more shoes. Unfortunately, she meant what she'd said; whenever I wore a skirt or a pair of dress pants, I had to sport the Top 10's to accommodate them. I had to sport my Top 10's with everything I wore…how embarrassing!

I still hung out with a few of my classmates back from middle school. We sat together during lunch hour, but I was always late because my locker was on the third floor. Every day before making my entrance to sit with Tanya, Macy, and Ty'Juan, my so-called friends, I could tell they were talking about me and laughing, but I played it off. I ignored it. Every Friday Diane gave me ten dollars for allowance and that included purchasing my lunch in the lunchroom for the week, because I wasn't eligible for free meals, so I stayed broke. The crew would treat me through the week, and when Friday rolled around I was eager to pay them back out of great appreciation. I'd walk in the lunchroom to the same unfaithful, sinister looks and giggles, but I continued to play it off. Anyway, it felt good paying them back for the times they treated me. After a while, I was tired of the fakeness, and I stopped hanging with them, because my self-esteem began to drop even more. I was still trying to conquer the demons from my past, and dealing with fake people wasn't helping. Although we were all close in middle school, I never believed then they were faithful to me. Thank God I never shared anything personal with them; there's no telling what they would have thought of me. I really had no self-esteem then, and that made me feel bad about myself. And wearing the same shoes with every outfit made me look and feel even worse.

3

'Til Death Do Us Part

The phone rang and Diane answered and listened to the deep voice on the other end of the line asking to speak with her; the voice not familiar. "Who is this? How do you know my name? Have we met before?" He made up some story that Diane obviously didn't remember, so she hung up. He called again and again, cracking little friendly jokes, and eventually she gave in. They communicated over the phone for about two months before she finally decided to welcome him into our home, and eventually the short visits turned in to a permanent stay. T'mone was short, dark, and cocky—built, with a very low haircut, well-groomed, with dark features and cocked eyes. His spirit however, was dark and beguiling; I absolutely could not believe Diane moved him in and as quick as she did. Whenever our family came to visit, he'd go straight upstairs to the bedroom without speaking. He never invited his family members over nor did they call; he never once took Diane to meet any of them.

The phone rang. Derf said: "How does your mom like my uncle?"

"What?" I said. Derf was the one who gave our number to T'mone. He wanted them to hook up, but he also said, "Your mama's going to end up killing him, I'm telling you!" While he was laughing hilariously, I was thinking to myself, *What kinda plan's this negro got that's gonna result in Diane killing him?* Which she definitely didn't have a problem doing, but I didn't tell Derf that.

T'mone and I didn't get along. He never said anything to me and vice versa; something about him wasn't right. He was trouble; if there was something he didn't like about me, he would go to Diane and he chose the punishment. I was never an A-student. That stopped after I started getting raped and kept it bottled up. Now all of a sudden when I came home from school with a bad grade, my punishments were harsh and cruel, I mean from one card marking to the next. That was a quarter of a year with no TV, radio, phone, company, or outdoors.

The Christmas holiday was my favorite season of the year. I usually spent it at Nina's house, because her siblings were all close in age and that made Christmas all the merrier. Being an only child, spending Christmas alone was boring for me. Diane used to buy me all these board games like checkers, Monopoly, and Life. Who the heck were my opponents? She didn't play any board games with me. This Christmas holiday, I was bummed out. My childhood past continued to haunt me, and I continuously felt weird and abnormal; nothing had changed. Diane began neglecting me and was growing mean. Her entire persona had changed.

I can't remember what petty thing T'mone did that caused Diane to yell at me, but whatever it was, I was totally fed up. He started yelling at me too, and once he was done I walked away quickly and didn't say a word, because I didn't want to be disrespectful. He didn't care about my well-being; he just wanted me out of the way and on punishment twenty-four/ seven. That way Diane and I would never spend quality time together and he could have her all to himself and attain dominancy over the entire house. T'mone ran up on me, lifting me into the air by my neck, choking the life out of me, and Diane just stood there. That negro hadn't lived with us two months and already he was puttin' the hands to me. If we had known him nine years, he still had no right physically chastising me. I always thought a mother should chastise her daughter; if it were my dad, I would have felt differently. He wouldn't have choked me, he would've chastised me out of love. That was something T'mone didn't have—love.

T'mone said, "Go over to Nina's house for the holiday and you better not be a day late coming home!"

I cried angrily because I couldn't believe what had just happened. Diane allowed him to put his hands on me, and my daddy was nowhere to be found because I hadn't talked to him in a while. I missed my daddy. I needed him!

I banged my foot on the corner of the wall. T'mone was sitting in the kitchen, smoking on a cigar pipe. He asked if he could take a look, so I sat down—not that I wanted to, but I was interested in knowing what his intentions were. I was also hoping I could bring peace in the home for the love of Diane. He grabbed my foot and laid it on his penis and began slightly massaging himself with my foot like I didn't notice. I felt the heat and the rise coming on. Immediately I started having flashbacks. I wanted to kill him; it felt so gross. Instantly I jumped up, quickly walking out of the kitchen. I went to my room and locked the door. I made a vow to myself to open my mouth if ever I ended up in a gruesome situation like this.

The very next morning I saw Diane in the kitchen. T'mone was in the bedroom. I immediately told her, and no she didn't brush off the situation in denial. Wow! She had the audacity to tell me he was only trying to help. "No, Mama, he wasn't." She totally ignored me, walked out the kitchen, and strolled straight up the stairs. I felt so alone with no one to talk to, and had now lost my sense of security. I didn't know how to reach out to anyone other than Diane whenever I went through anything, bad or good. I was grateful that it was the only and last time I encountered that situation with T'Mone. More than likely Diane didn't say anything to him; there's no telling what would have taken place as dark and evil as T'mone was.

Finally, I was off punishment. I was tired of Nina and Crystal walking past my house, teasing me, "Shinice, when you gone get them shackles off your feet, giirrl?" laughing their butts off. How embarrassing. It was like every time Diane moved a man in, they treated me like Cinderella. One of her ex's used to have a vegetable garden full of freakin' tomatoes that his daughter and I had to boil, peel, and stew in jars, it seemed like every day. I was sick of it. During my punishments I used my spare time to exercise my creativity, which I had no idea I was blessed with. I started writing poems and making recipes with a twist of my own touch, and presentation was a must. Both talents came so easily to me that I became a whiz, but didn't have the concept of transitioning my talents into something major. Everyone loved my poems and my cooking.

Even though I introduced Nina and Crystal, when I was on punishment they would hang out and became closer. When my punishment was over we hung out every day, doing what a lot of teenagers did best—skipping school, smoking, and drinking.

Eventually we started having sex with boys. I guess being sexually molested by people who were much older than me caused me to affiliate myself with older men. I was only fourteen when I started having sex with a nineteen-year-old guy named Maleek. Nina introduced me, because her boyfriend and Maleek were boys.

I started sneaking him in through the side door. The possibility of me being raped never crossed my mind. I believe it was because I was willful; it was my choice to allow this man in my secret garden. My body and mind were full of sexual desire. The feeling of his erectness massaging my vaginal walls as he slowly glided inside of me made me forget how I was mentally affected in the past. The sex was awesome, because I had a choice in the matter. I was in control, and I was on top. I made sure it remained that way; it was therapeutic for my wanting to have a normal sex life without feeling violated. I was the best cowgirl born.

Sneaking Maleek in my house lasted about two weeks until Diane heard a soft knock at the side door. She grabbed her .357 and pointed it at him through the upstairs window and he took off like a crack-head who hit a major lick. As soon as Diane gave me that blank look, my jaws started flappin' immediately. I always had a good habit of telling the truth, like when Nina and I were stopped by the police for jay-walking. I gave them my full government name, but Nina made one up. She thought that was hilarious, because I had to pay for my ticket and she didn't. Telling the truth to Diane at the top of the staircase about Maleek got me knocked down to the bottom.

Early afternoon we were knocking on Maleek's door. His mother answered and let us in as if she already knew why we were there. There Maleek stood, along with Nina's boyfriend and the rest of the crew. Diane pulled out her .357 and made it firmly clear that if she caught them at her side door again, she would kill them. Later that afternoon we all got together and we laughed and laughed.

Although Crystal, Nina, and I were close, I never shared much of anything with them, because I didn't trust anybody and especially them. I knew they weren't faithful friends, but I still hung around anyway. Even though Diane knew my past, I still needed counseling, because she never went through the motions with me. She made sure I never had any encounters with my molesters or any other. However, she never asked how I felt about what I had gone through, and she never counseled me. I just wanted to feel and live a normal life like all the other teenagers; I always felt different. The memories were always there and I continued to have low self-esteem. I felt self-conscious about things I said, did, and even the way I dressed and walked. I had pretty clothes, but didn't have fashionable ideas as to coordinate style. The only thing Nina and Crystal knew about me was my everyday life with them. The only thing they knew about my past was me bopping my head up and down on the pillow with the radio blasting in my ear. I really didn't care if they saw me, because it had become therapeutic in my life. My imagination was my reality, like Gabourey Sidibe in "Precious".

Diane had a twin brother, Damon, who was incarcerated. He used to live with us until Diane beat down his side-chick. He grabbed our garbage can from the backyard and threw it through our picture window. I don't know if Diane pressed charges on him or not. I just know she put him out.

Damon had gotten himself into some trouble as usual, so Diane dropped me off at Nina's, then went to visit with him. When she returned home T'mone was furious and beat her for three hours straight. Her right eye was bruised purple and so swollen that her sunglasses could barely fit on her face.

The next morning Diane filed a police report and got a restraining order against him. The officer told her if T'mone came to the house to notify them immediately, because he still had a set of keys. Diane also said the officer told her if T'mone comes back to the house and they don't make it in time, oh well..."

Diane continued on to work and the day was going well until T'mone pulled up and asked her to meet him on Mount Elliot and Palmer. A few of her friends that lived on her route walked over to make sure she was okay. She had already put them up on what happened the night before. She really didn't have a choice; it was evident. She also wanted to make sure she had eyewitnesses while on the job. Of course she didn't agree to meet T'mone alone, because she didn't know what to expect after what had already taken place. When he pulled off, Diane thought: *Mount Elliot and Palmer? That's the Trinity Cemetery!* She drove straight to the police station after leaving work and reported him showing up on her route. She then went home and hadn't been there a half hour when T'mone arrived on her front porch threatening to use the key to come in. She told him not to come in or she would shoot. He told her she didn't have the heart and used that house key for the last time. Like the officer said, "Oh well!"

Police surrounded the block only to see T'mone lying in a pool of blood from two shots to the chest. The power from Diane's .357 had thrown him right back out of the house. He flew right out of his shoes, tied up and all; they were left sitting in the hallway where he took his first and last step inside. The vast crowd surrounded the block in a bombshell as Diane came out of the house handcuffed. Two hours later Diane was released on self-defense. T'mone's sister threatened to retaliate. Diane said: *"I can send you with your brother; it'll be my pleasure."*

I resided with Nina and her family until things calmed down. I wasn't too adamant about coming home and viewing T'mone's body structure outlined in white chalk on the pavement. Thank God that it looked as if nothing ever happened once I arrived. I went upstairs to my room, trying to submerge the horrific incident until I heard Diane calling me. Before I could enter her room, she said, *"Shinice, look!"* There was a hole drilled through her closet wall behind where his clothes hung, straight into my bedroom. Diane had me go into my room and stand in front of where the hole was drilled, which was straight through an uncovered electrical socket. She looked through the hole, only seeing me from the waist down. Her blood boiled over; she probably had a flashback of when I tried telling her what T'Mone did to me.

Diane exclaimed, *"If I knew where he was buried, I'd dig him up and kill him again,"* more than likely at the Trinity Cemetery, where he probably had plans on digging a hole for her.

4
Suffering The Consequences

Shortly after Diane killed T'Mone, she left the post office and applied for disability. The tragedy changed her mentally, to the extent that she began thinking she had an odor; she said she could smell herself. I told her it wasn't true and so did her loved ones, but she didn't believe any of us. Every time somebody rubbed their nose around her, she thought it was because of her.

As for me, I began to get on the wild side, hanging out with a group of girls up the block: Naomi, Laurie, and her cousin Gina. Laurie and I walked home from school together and we always met up with Gina and Naomi so we could all hang out. However, Laurie and Gina were crack-heads. They didn't use pipes; they crushed crack up in Zigzag papers. We were hanging out at a crack-house one night when I decided to take my first hit. Immediately I started sipping liquor in hopes of leveling out my high before it even hit; I was scared, I didn't know what to expect. I looked down and noticed my skin had flared up like crocodile skin. My entire body rashed out, excluding my face; I was so glad no one else saw it. Immediately I walked out of the house without uttering a word.

I was two blocks from home but it felt like two miles, and my heart pounded from paranoia because I didn't know what was going on with me. The only thought running through my head was *Please don't let me die!* I was so glad my favorite uncle lived with us at the time. Uncle Myron was a Detroit police officer. He was my confidant; I could trust him to keep a secret.

He rushed me to the hospital. The doctor said I had an allergic reaction, but didn't know to what, because I didn't tell him. I could've died that night, taking my first hit. Thank God crack wasn't a part of my journey in life. I could've easily gotten addicted had I not had the reaction. I made it my business not to ever touch crack again and never told another soul.

Laurie and Gina continued to be crack-heads, hanging out at the park, trickin' to feed their habit. By the time I was walking out the door for school, they were walking up the block in the opposite direction looking a hot mess from turning tricks all night. I began to ease away from that environment. Then one day Laurie saw Nina in the bathroom and made up all kinds of lies that I allegedly said about Nina. Nina fed into it purposely to tell Laurie gossip I used to say about her. Laurie was just a chick up the block I was cool with, but Nina was my girl. It seemed like every time I hung out with anybody other than Nina, she didn't like them or some kind of way some mess got started, like it did between me and Laurie.

After school Naomi, Laurie, and Gina jumped me in the doorway of my house, while Nina and Crystal laughed hilariously over the phone. They kept telling me not to let them in, but Laurie was already standing in the doorway. We were already talking about the he-said-she-said situation, but then when Naomi and Gina walked up, they all jumped me. I was surprised at Naomi, because we grew up together, she didn't really know Laurie and Gina, and didn't really care for them like that; that's what happens when you trust broads. Again, I was the one who introduced Naomi to the girls. When Diane came home from work she went to all their homes and threatened them in front of their relatives. Naomi apologized after a few days and then the rest followed behind, but I still continued to keep away from that crowd. As for Nina, I continued being her friend like the lil' naïve and gullible girl I was.

I told Diane there were apparitions of T'Mone in the house. Every night I'd get up and grab late night snacks from the fridge, and a black shadow of T'Mone would appear on the stairs, watching me. When I turned my head the other way and glanced back at the stairs, he was gone, but once I started up the stairs to head back to my room, I could hear him walking behind me. I'd stop walking and turn around quickly to see if I saw him, but I didn't. I only heard his footsteps behind me.

Diane was in denial, but I guess I would've been too if I was the one who killed him. Having no thought of moving out—not that Diane would've allowed me to—I had no choice but to put my fears behind me and deal with it. There's an old saying that wherever a person dies, there is where the spirit dwells. However, T'mone didn't die in the house; he died shortly after arriving at the hospital. Although the power from the .357 threw him right out of his shoes, they were left sitting in the hallway, tied up perfectly as if they were still on his feet.

I noticed after the death of T'Mone three fingernail scratches were deeply engraved in the stone décor that surrounded the front door, and they were thick like nails of a gargoyle, as if they were determined not to leave the house. These scratches weren't the norm, but as if they were from far beyond this world; that's when Diane changed maliciously.

Diane and I had a terrible fallout; I mean, she could say things that were a straight jab to the heart. She was good for calling me the b-word and screaming out she hated me. I felt so desecrated, because she was my mother, my rock, all I had and trusted, and I loved her. Jaden was someone I dated, nothing serious, and he always told me if I ever needed a place to stay, just come, so I was in need of taking his advice. Our house phone was disconnected, so I couldn't call Jaden to prepare him for my coming unexpectedly. C'eno happened to come by in the midst of all the commotion and cries. He attended the same high school as me. The timing was perfect, because I needed transportation to Jaden's house.

C'eno took me to a motel. Although I knew him from school and he'd drop by the house from time to time, I was still leery. I had no idea we were going to a motel. I mean, what motive was behind taking me there other than taking advantage of me sexually? I was hoping he would comfort me, considering we had established somewhat of a friendship, and the fact of him popping up in the midst of the chaos and seeing me crying.

C'eno asked what had happened between me and Diane, while at the same time, cracking open a bottle of E&J and rolling up a joint. I turned my back to him as I began sharing my dilemma, and daydreaming at the television screen. Not once did he make a response when I was done talking. An uncomfortable emptiness filled the room. I turned around to see C'eno lying across the bed, stroking his rock-hard penis. He didn't care about my problems; his only intentions were to take advantage of my being in a vulnerable state of mind and respond to me sexually instead of being the friend I needed at that time. My situation reminded me of Fantasia's life story; she knew the guy from school, but didn't really know him-know him and he took advantage of her. Somewhat my situation didn't surprise me; it had become a part of my life repetitiously. C'eno forced me to undress. "You gone give it up or all yo s*** in the trunk of my car goin' wit' me and you'll be stranded."

My mind was hollow, not to add how weak and wasted I was from all the crying, drinking, and smoking. Cell phones weren't popping then, and I knew he was much stronger than me, so I felt helpless and clueless. I knew he would beat the brakes off me, take my belongings, and leave me stranded if I didn't give him what he wanted; I could feel it. I didn't have one penny in my pocket. Once the intoxication took over, I saw the demon in him. Fear took over in me.

C'eno reached in his pocket for a condom, put it on, and drilled his penis into me right away, and instantly I had flashbacks of my childhood. I couldn't understand why sexual abuse seemed to be an essential part of my life or why I made such senseless choices. I just laid there with my eyes glued to the ceiling daydreaming, soaked in tears, blaming myself for everything. I began to cry silently in pain with my eyes tightly squeezed shut, and not just from C'eno pounding inside of me, but all that had occurred in my life. I was affected physically, emotionally, and mentally; I was a lost child. I already had a feeling I was pregnant, and this punk was just pounding inside of me like it was his first time having sex.

Eventually C'eno dropped me off at Jaden's house, and had the nerve to wait and see if someone answered the door. I banged and I banged for fifteen minutes, but no one ever answered. There I stood, looking and feeling like a fool. *Should I get back in the car with this negro or find an alley to sleep in?* I looked back at C'eno and he pulled off intensely. I was left stuck-stupid, standing there with what I felt was my entire life stuffed in garbage bags. I was definitely the prototype of a bag lady. I reluctantly knocked on the neighbor's door and asked if I could use the phone; I was extremely ashamed. How was I going to explain to Diane that I had no idea where C'eno lived or his government name? I wasn't thinking. I felt so stupid! I didn't know the day would turn out the way it did.

Diane pulled up still angered, but at least she showed up. She took me straight to the hospital to have me checked out for any STDs. Thank God all the tests came back negative, however, I was six weeks pregnant and Diane went ballistic. I thought she would've at least appreciated her only daughter being safe from any STDs, but that didn't faze her. She made it clear that I wasn't bringing my child into the world just like the first time. I was first pregnant at the age of fifteen, messing around with some "Ready For The World" looking dude. What an unattractive memory. He used to pounce when he walked so his soggy, dripping, greasy jerry curls swung from side to side. I didn't feel he was a significant part of my life, so I left this story out. Our relationship lasted the length of his jerry curl...short!

The bottom line was I had no intentions of aborting my child the second time around. I was eighteen. I felt I needed this child, because he or she would love me unconditionally. I needed someone to love and someone to love me back genuinely. I was yearning for love and I was destined to get it someway, somehow. Diane made it clear that I was to get out of her house. I started searching for a place to live.

Cinderella and I had the same curfew—midnight. My God I was eighteen already! I called Diane for a ride, because Jaden and his friend who drove left early, and I wanted to stay close to curfew. I tried keeping space between Diane and me, because we didn't get along at all. Usually Jaden would call me a cab, use his mother's car or his brother would take me home, but I was unfortunate this time. I waited outside for Diane as I was fifteen minutes late past my curfew. When she arrived she got out of the car, walked over to me, and punched me in the face while I was pregnant and all. I slipped on the ice, but was able to keep balance and not fall to the ground. Like I said, usually I had a ride, but this time I had no choice but to call her, because waiting on a bus would've gotten me home really late. I rarely called Diane at all. I only called on her whenever my back was against the wall. Diane used everything I shared with her and experienced in my life to manipulate, and instill control and fear in me. I didn't know how to reach out to anyone else or know enough to survive alone and make wise decisions and she knew that.

Diane had me where she wanted me. She made it her business to destroy any relationship I had with older women, like my friends' mothers. Ladondra's mother passed on to Glory when she was a child. Diane didn't care about my relationship with Nina's mom, because we didn't have a close relationship. Diane only focused on the ones I was close to; ones who tried to be in my corner. What I mean by that is: I didn't really know how to reach out for help, but whenever I did, the genuine ones were there. They were concerned, and knew Diane was an unstable and miserable woman. Her relationships never worked out; they always ended disastrously. It made her feel complete to take all her frustrations out on me, which I didn't understand. Instead of her teaching me the facts of life, she manipulated my mind to accommodate her unstable ways. I didn't understand anything.

After that blow to the face from Diane, I moved out! I moved in with L.C. and his mother. L.C. was a mutual friend of me and Jaden. Every day Jaden came by, playing baby daddy, pretending he cared. I remembered his words, "Anytime you need a place to stay, you can stay with me." I echoed those same words back to him earlier that same day before Diane picked me up. I told Jaden what happened to me that night. He had words of compassion, but no emotions whatsoever; I thought he would have some concern considering I was pregnant with our first child. I expected him to quote those words to me again that I was in need of hearing, but he didn't. I allowed him to treat me like I had no respect or dignity for myself, because I didn't. I didn't know who I was or how I was supposed to be treated; I just didn't know!

Jaden couldn't offer me a place to stay. He lived with his brothers and had no say so, and more than likely he didn't want to be tied down to no baby mama, but I didn't think about that.

L.C., Lena, and I decided to stop by Jaden's house; we were all headed over to L.C.'s cousin's house to hang out. There I was again, banging on the side door and again no answer, so I walked away, but Lena stood there banging. Eventually Jaden came to the door with his penis peeking through the curtain first. Lena pulled me down the driveway. We strolled up the block as she was yelling and cussing, and all I could do was shake my head.

We were having a good time at L.C.'s cousin's house, in the basement, talking and laughing. After a while Lena had to leave and pick her little brother up from school and kept stressing for me to come with her, but I was tired of walking and I was pregnant, so she went on.

Twenty minutes later Jaden came over, stuntin' wit' his boys. He walked straight up to me and said, *"What are you doing over here acting like a slut?"* L.C., his cousin and I looked at Jaden, stunned. He knew being a slut wasn't of my nature, but because he was caught and exposed with his penis out, he decided to run the guilt trip on me. I was fully dressed, wearing a long-sleeve, knee-length blue jean dress snapped from the neck down, that Lena let me wear. Not only did Jaden snatch the dress off me, but he did it right in front of his boys. My body went twirling like a tornado.

Jaden said: *"Her dress will be lying in the furnace room when y'all done,"* and out the door he went, leaving his crew standing there. L.C. and his cousin didn't say a word. They were afraid of standing up to Jaden and all those boys they didn't even know.

Jaden's clique turned into hungry wolves and they started drooling from the mouth. Unbelievably, L.C. and his cousin were the first two to tell the boys to let them hit it first. L.C. threw me on the bed and then his cousin closed the door. The other six stood on the other side of the door yelling impatiently, *"Hurry up, man, so we can hit dat too!"* I was flabbergasted and crying hysterically. I have to honestly say, I was in total shock. *"L.C. what are you doing?"*

He got on top of me with his clothes on and placed a quilt over us and whispered, *"Keep crying until we can figure out something because it's too many of them!"* Jaden's boys were like wolves on the other side of that door.

I lay there frantically looking up at the ceiling again. I couldn't think. I was petrified. All of a sudden *"Boom"* the door went flying open and L.C.'s cousin flew against the wall and L.C. had the look of great fear in his eyes as if he was next in line. All we saw was a herd of hungry wolves charging at me, drooling from the mouth. They came charging like a football team in tackling motion. I screamed! Everything went black.

I woke up to everybody facing the wall handcuffed. My heart was still racing and my face swollen from the tears it absorbed. As I explained in a few words to the police how L.C. and his cousin tried to protect me, Lena came running in the side door straight to the basement. *"WHAT HAPPENED? OH*

MY GOD, WHAT HAPPENED?" She lost it and from there she started swinging on every last one of those boys. It took three officers to remove her from the basement, but she kept running in again and again.

The police asked if I wanted to press charges and I said no, simply because they hadn't raped me; they didn't get a chance to, thank God. I gave them Jaden's name. When they all came charging in on me, I blacked out only for a few seconds before police arrived; I knew I hadn't been raped. Although I didn't know Jesus, something in my spirit led me to give the situation to him. Vengeance was his, and I trusted he was going to handle it. I hoped it would be a life's learned lesson for those guys in the future ahead. There were enough brothers prison-bound from unwise choices and/or being in the wrong place at the wrong time; they deserved a second chance. Had they touched me, yes, I would have pressed charges, but I didn't want to lie out of anger, and then have to answer to God. You never know how that situation may have changed their lives for the better. I forgave them!

I told Diane and Uncle Myron what happened, and they went on a hunt immediately looking for Jaden! Diane may have been mentally abusive to me, but she definitely didn't allow anyone else to mistreat me. The first stop was Jaden's mother's house, and of course he wasn't there. Diane said: *"Tell him we're looking for him,"* and my uncle Myron stood there quietly, dressed in everyday clothing, never saying a word.

The same evening I met up with Jaden over at his boy's house. I didn't tell Diane or my uncle Myron because I knew they had it out for him, and I guess I did it out of love for his unborn son. I know it sounds crazy, but I wanted my child to get a chance to meet his dad when actually, I shouldn't have really cared. The no-good butt-hole tried to set me up to get raped with his unborn son inside me. A situation such as this is what made me ask myself "what the heck was wrong with me!" Why did I make such unstable decisions; I didn't have an answer. I needed to ask him face-to-face why he would do something so scandalous. I was the mother of his son. Jaden knew what happened to me at the hotel and I was pregnant with his son then…why? He told me that because I caught him cheating, he flipped the script because he felt guilty. What a loser!

After all that had taken place, Diane decided to let me move back in. I also knew there was something beneficial in it for her. It wasn't in Diane's character to do anything motherly for me unless something was in it for her. I moved back. L.C. had four younger siblings and I was sleeping on the sofa, so I knew soon I would need private space for me and the baby, and as for Jaden, he went to jail, but when he was released he contacted me immediately. Although he feared coming by the house, he was destined to apologize to me, Diane, and my uncle Myron. I saw the demonic look on Diane's face. I had to pull her aside and beg her again to please chill out for the love of her first grandchild.

Jaden acknowledged his son to me and his family, but not in the presence of his friends, but they knew Daevon was his child. Daevon was a spitting image of Jaden's mother. It really didn't matter what Jaden thought, because I was done with him after putting me and his unborn child through what he put us through. I just needed to see him one more time, because I needed to know why! I continued on with my life, raising my son as a single parent. I took it upon myself to visit with Jaden's mother every Sunday so she could spend time with her grandson and we could get to know her better. Eventually I was tired of being the only one trying to make an effort for her to have a relationship with her grandson. I stopped the visits.

Jaden's mother never called or came by; she showed no concern whatsoever. She and Jaden's siblings were the main ones talking about how Daevon looked just like them and Jaden was a poor excuse for a father, but none of them made any effort to be a part of his life. The only family member who did the best she could to show concern for Daevon was Jaden's sister Becky. As for Jaden and the rest of the family, I never contacted them for anything. Becky asked that I not treat her like a stranger, and if ever I needed anything for Daevon to give her a call, but I never did. I forgave Jaden for all he put me and his son through, and I forgave his mother for not being that loving grandmother that every child deserves.

> *...for I, the Lord your God, am a jealous God,*
> *punishing the children for the sin of the*
> *parents to the third and fourth generation*
> *of those who hate me.*
> *Exodus 20:5*

5
Getting Acquainted to The One Who Conceived Me

Diane met a new friend named Princeton; he was tall, dark, and muscular with a bald head. Uncle Damon introduced them. He was dating Princeton's sister. Here Diane did it again, moving a guy in after only knowing him a few months. By this time Uncle Damon was living with us. Uncle Myron had long moved out; he only moved in to help Diane get financially stable.

Diane's friend explained to her how we could receive benefits from the state: checks, food stamps, medical benefits, WIC, and everything else that the state had to offer. We called her Southfield Sherry because she lived in Southfield, MI, and Diane had two other friends with the same name. I was eligible for one hundred fifty dollars that I would receive twice a month. I was also eligible for three hundred dollars in food stamps, medical, and WIC benefits.

Once Daevon turned three months, I started feeding him jar food, and bought enough to carry him for the month, but Diane put all that to a stop. Princeton wasn't contributing anything and neither was my uncle Damon. He was receiving over a hundred dollars in food stamps, and Diane allowed him to keep them all to himself. Uncle Damon had a heck of a hustle, sitting in a wheelchair panhandling all day. Diane had the audacity to tell me that I could no longer purchase Daevon jar food with my food stamps because we had too many mouths to feed. Her mortgage was just over three hundred, and I was responsible for half, and one-third of my cash benefits were automatically deducted for the lights and gas each pay. I had to provide all necessities for myself and Daevon, including his baby food, with cash.

I started blending fresh fruits and vegetables in the blender for Daevon. I had to make do with what I had. Actually blending fresh food was much healthier for him anyway, because that's how it was done back during slavery. I had to hand wash clothes on an old-school washing board because Diane was being cheap and didn't wanna get the washing machine repaired.

By the time I paid the majority of the bills, I was left with twenty dollars. I had to live off that for two weeks and hadn't purchased any hygienic products for myself. If we ran low on food before the month was out, I was forced to come out of my pocket to add to what Diane had. I knew if I took on a job, she would've vamped my entire check. I would've ended up in the same situation, so what was the point in working for nothing? Diane was determined to stay in control of me.

I started shoplifting, because twenty dollars wasn't going to cut it for me; I did what I felt I had to do at that time. Every pay I made it my business to buy an outfit for Daevon and then steal one, placing it in his diaper bag. I then proceeded on to another store to shoplift for things I needed.

I started messing around with the Chaldean who owned the liquor store five blocks away to make ends meet. I may have lost my dignity, but knowing that he wasn't a married man made me feel like I had some decency about myself; A married man, I could never do. I used to lie to Diane, telling her I found money walking up the block. I had to tell her something, because she was deep in my business. That was her way of staying in control of me. She was always questioning me whenever I came walking in the house with shopping bags. She had me fully under her control and had manipulated my mind to the point where I didn't know how to think for myself.

Although it was a struggle keeping food on the table, I still gave food to a family that was in need. I had five pounds of chicken wings and four cans of pork and beans; half for lunch and the other half for dinner. I was preparing the first half for lunch as I pranced back and forth to the front door, watching traffic and waiting for the chicken to finish frying. A white family driving in an old-school sky-blue station wagon turned on to the block and parked in front of my house as if they knew where they were going. I didn't think anything of it, considering there was a drug house right next door. Everybody who bought drugs from that house always parked in front of ours, you know how it is. I walked back to the kitchen and continued cooking, and that's when I heard the knock at the door. *"We're hungry and we were wondering if you had any food?"* There stood a mother, father, and three young children who I assumed were theirs. I was honored to help them; I hadn't a second thought on where my family's next meal was coming from.

I asked if they had a stove to prepare the food, because I would've given them what I had already prepared, but fortunately they did have appliances. I gave them all we had, our dinner, and they were so grateful. We had no more food in the house other than the lunch I had just prepared, and I wasn't worried, not one bit. I never saw them again. If I stand correctly I believe I was entertaining angels.

Everybody in the house got along good except for Diane and me. She started treating me more and more like a broad in the streets. As I mentioned before, she never allowed me to get too close to anybody, and if I did, she would do everything in her power to destroy it. Diane's everyday agenda was to keep me isolated from reality so I'd stay dependent upon her, so I wouldn't know how to survive without her. Every time she got upset with me, she stole my welfare checks, and then would have the audacity to ask if I needed to borrow money. When check time rolled around again, I'd end up owing her every dime. I began selling my body regularly to the Chaldean, derogating my dignity and pride; my womanhood.

When Diane worked for the post office, she was the mail carrier on my Dad's block, and that's how they met. When she couldn't get her way with him, she'd steal his VA checks and he'd have to wait another month. I've actually watched her smear cigarette ashes on people's mail. It was her way of making it dingy and dirty so it looked as if it had gotten lost outside somewhere, and someone found it, stuck back in the mail for redelivery.

As usual, our phone was disconnected so I had to use the neighbor's phone. I called a friend so I could get out of the house and get some fresh air. I walked back to go get Daevon and I dressed because we were leaving within the next hour. Here came Diane out of the blue. *"You're not going anywhere."* I didn't even bother to ask why, because I knew she was just being evil. I rushed back to the neighbor's to try reaching my friend before she wasted gas coming my way.

When I came back home, Diane was standing in the doorway. *"Go upstairs. I'm going to show you who's boss around here. I said you can't go out."* I tried explaining to her that I didn't go anywhere, I was trying to reach my friend before she headed my way. Diane didn't listen to a word I said; she just snatched me by my collar and started tagging my face. I didn't have a choice but to endure it. I wouldn't dare raise my hand at the woman who gave birth to me. I had nowhere else to go and I had no money. I still didn't have much of a relationship with my dad, because of Diane. I was just stuck right where she wanted me. I had to deal with it, because I knew no way out. When my uncle Damon saw my face, he went off on Diane. She scratched me up pretty bad, and I had a few scuff marks on my cheekbones.

Princeton was a cool, laid-back guy and an attentive listener when you needed someone to talk to, and he made the best mac and cheese with the famous Focus Hope block cheese. Every day Princeton, Diane, and I played Monopoly or cards, talking and laughing. Princeton made Diane happy and that kept her off my back, just a little, but she still continued to control me, use me, and talk about me like a dog.

Princeton took me to Belle Isle, and for the first time I got a chance to grip Diane's sports car. He looked troubled and I wasn't used to that; he was always so jazzy and laid back. Princeton faced me and asked if he could confide in me something personal; if I could keep a secret, and I said *"Of course"*. He goes on *"When your uncle Damon told me he wanted me to meet someone and brought me over to the house, I thought I was being introduced to you, not your mother. I'm moving out. I can't live with both of you, sleeping with one, but in love with the other."*

My heart sank to the pit of my stomach. I knew something like this was going to break Diane's heart and add even more strain to our relationship as mother and daughter, because she loved Princeton so much.

Not in a million years would I have ever thought Princeton felt the way he did. Not once did I sense any sign of him being attracted to me. I never saw Princeton look at me sexually or like he had any interest whatsoever. I despised that very moment, because I was the focal point of the situation. I knew I would have to be the one to tell Diane the heartbreaking news. There was no way I could keep something like that from her, watching her bounce around happy every day, knowing that their relationship was a lie. I told Princeton that I couldn't live with myself if I kept a secret like that from my own mother. He said, *"I understand, but just wait until the morning to tell her; I'll be gone."*

Princeton was gone before I woke up, and there sat Diane at the table in the breakfast room. It took everything in me to tell Diane the bad news, I mean everything in me! I took a deep breath and let it all out, word for word. I saw the discomforting look on her face, and no response. My mind was all over the place. What if I hadn't told her and just let Princeton make up a lie as to why their relationship couldn't work out? It would have torn me up inside for hiding the truth, and I couldn't live with that. Diane walked out of the kitchen, back downstairs to her bedroom. I was full of distress, and the pit of my stomach was all buckled up inside me. I didn't know how she felt or what was next, and that troubled me very deeply.

I prepared lunch for Daevon. Diane was still in her room. I guess she was mentally drained, so I expected her to still be sleeping, but I had made her some lunch too. I was hoping I could relieve some of the pain and agony she was feeling.

I walked in her bedroom slowly making my way closer to her, when I noticed she was lying on her back, foaming at the mouth. Something led me to her bathroom, and there lay open an empty pill bottle; Diane had taken a drug overdose of Tylenol 3's.

I panicked and ran upstairs to tell my uncle Damon and

then immediately ran to the neighbor's house and dialed 911.
This was Diane's third suicide attempt. The previous ones happened when I was a baby, according to a few family members
and friends.

I watched Diane as she lay there in the ICU attached to a
breathing machine, and IV needles stuck in the crease of her
arms. I sat there relentlessly blaming myself for her actions; all
kinds of thoughts ran through my mind. If I hadn't said anything, she wouldn't have been in that predicament, I thought. I
just knew I wouldn't be able to live with myself if I kept something like that from my own mother.

Diane was in a coma for nearly two months. Her kidneys
had completely shut down, and she was on life support the entire time. The family and I shared visiting hours, rotating, not
leaving her side, hoping she would fight for her life and revive
from a coma. I was a nervous wreck; I prayed myself tired day
in and day out, knowing the doctor said that it didn't look
good. I didn't know what to think or do. Diane was all I knew.
I didn't feel like I would've knew how to survive without her.

My aunt Candice and godmother Nia were at Diane's bed-
side before, and when she came out of the coma. The doctor
examined her and still it wasn't looking good at all. I was called
to come to the hospital right away. I looked down at Diane
as she lay there extremely weak and still not able to talk. She
wrote her words on a notepad. *"Be strong, I need you to breathe
for me and take care of Daevon."* I broke out in tears and walked
out with that paper; I kept it close to my heart. I tried to stay
strong and began to become very prayerful, taking it one day
at a time.

Princeton called. I told him what happened and not once
did he seem to have the slightest concern or attempt to pay
a visit. I suppose he felt he was to blame for it, and probably

thought his presence would finish killing her off.

As time went by, Diane started recovering, thank God; she was released after being in the hospital for three months. Unbelievably, the minute Diane stepped into the house, the devil jumped right inside of her. She cussed me out for rearranging the furniture, which I did to accommodate her so she wouldn't have to strain going up and down the stairs. Diane had become extremely evil toward me, more than ever before. We had everything set up for her convenience, and she didn't even appreciate that. All she did was cuss, cuss, and cuss some more, but only at me. Every time she called my name, she sounded possessed. I literally heard a demon in her. Diane was worse off than she was before she was admitted to the hospital.

They will be divided, father against son and son against father, mother against daughter and daughter against mother.
Luke 12:53

6

In Bondage

I met Gino during the time Diane was hospitalized. He was a welter-weight boxer. Gino had a rock-hard body, very well built, with shoulder-length dreadlocks and an alluring Jamaican accent that would draw any woman's attention. He always stopped by to see me before he left for his daily workout at the gym, because he was only a block away.

Gino and I had gotten very well acquainted. Other than my attraction to his well-built, structured body and Jamaican accent, I enjoyed his company. We went out to dinner almost every night, getting to know one another without any distractions from Diane. Gino took good care of me, giving me money to go shopping and making sure I kept money in my pocket. Even though I was attracted to some qualities, I didn't have the same interest in Gino as he in me. I made sure we had that understanding before the showering of the gifts, because I didn't want to lead him on in any way.

Playing hard to get only caused Gino to come on to me even stronger. Every so often I hid out at Nina's to dodge him, but she and her sisters gave me away every time. The same qualities that attracted me were attractive to them as well; *"Giirrl, you betta snatch dat man up."* I was never a money-hungry person. I just did what I had to do to make ends meet, but I didn't wanna do it with Gino. However, listening to Nina-n-em, and Gino's persistence eventually lead me to give in. I slowly cut all ties with the Chaldean.

Seven months in, Gino and I were still dating. Diane seemed to like him and she allowed him to move in on account of me; it's obvious the fruit didn't fall far from the tree. It was no reason in particular I wanted Gino to move in besides the fact of me being lonely I guess. Gino worked as a cook at a steak restaurant and was able to get me hired in too. He continued to box, but worked around his work schedule so he kept himself booked for fight rounds at least once a month. The more money we brought in, the more Diane had her hand out. Every other week she'd be sitting in the kitchen waiting for us to walk through the door with a "B**** Better Have My Money" look on her face; she was draining us.

Time went on, and still I wasn't in love, just content. Gino eased my pain and agony; he was my Calgon. I really adored the relationship he had with Daevon.

Knowing I wasn't in love with Gino, I made the foolish mistake of getting pregnant by him. That's when Diane freaked out again and told me I was having an abortion just like all the other times. For once I agreed, because I knew I hadn't planned on spending the rest of my life with Gino. When he came home from work I told him the news and he was so happy, but that happy face turned upside down when I told him I was having an abortion. That was when I saw the other side of Gino. He sucker - punched me in the nose. Blood gushed out everywhere. *"Oh, you gone have my baby!"*

I rushed back to the clinic to get that baby sucked out of me ASAP. The doctor performed an ultrasound, and whatever he saw lead him to walk out of the room in the midst of it. He re-entered the room with two more doctors, and that's when I then began to worry and asked questions.

Come to find out I was pregnant with identical twin boys; I was shocked, I was overwhelmed. I also have to admit that I wasn't adamant at all about aborting two babies. The doctor said an abortion would cost me eight hundred dollars. If I didn't take care of it before the end of the week, the price would go up, because I was going on eight weeks into the pregnancy. Stuck again, not knowing what to do or think, especially after Gino punched me, and although he begged for my forgiveness, how was I to know that he wouldn't do it again? So many thoughts trampled through my head. I thought about how we had been dating almost a full year and he had never laid a hand on me. I also thought of how blessed I was being pregnant with twins. Lastly, I looked at the situation as an opportunity to escape from Diane.

Diane was disgusted when I told her I was pregnant with twins, and I lied and said the doctor didn't recommend aborting twins so late into the pregnancy. I had to come up with something, because I knew she would come up with the money quick if she knew the truth. I didn't understand what made her think I would accept her money for the abortion when I had my own money; it wasn't going to make a difference in my decision either way. Gino, on the other hand, who was starting to look like a monkey to me by the way, kept apologizing for punching me in the nose. He begged and pleaded for me to feel the way he did about having his children, but I didn't. I didn't want kids by Gino. He kept promising me he was going to give his sons *"the world title."*

Diane grew more and more bitter each day, which was nothing new, besides putting more strain on me. Although our relationship started going sour after the tragic separation with her and T'Mone, it really took a turn for the worse after the Princeton situation. I guess I was in the way of all her relationships. I believed this time it was the other way around, that she had a crush on Gino. Diane was always in his face he-he-ha-ha, undressing him with her eyes from head to toe, and talking about me behind my back to him like; what mother does that to their own child?

All the money Gino and I were giving Diane could've been a security deposit on our own place, so that's what we did. We only moved four houses down the street, but so what, I was on my own. Diane went nuts when the day came for us to move; she was slowly losing control. She grabbed my arms, shaking me, screaming, and crying out that Gino was no good and I needed to come back home, because he was going to beat me. I never told Diane Gino hit me. I was curious as to why she would scream something out like that; maybe it was a mother's intuition. My concern was, if she felt that way all along, why did she allow him to move in, and why was she in his face all the time, and talking about me behind my back? I was stuck between a rock and hard place, baffled. I had a dysfunctional relationship with my own mother and hoping like heck Gino wasn't a woman-beater. I had to weigh my options, but at the time anything was better than dealing with Diane. I was completely desolated and overwhelmed with stress from the verbal, mental, and emotional abuse from her. She was the most vindictive, scandalous, and controlling woman I'd ever laid eyes on. I had only one altercation with Gino the entire time we had been together, and that included no arguments. I'm not saying what he did was acceptable, but I needed so desperately to get away from Diane and find my own way in life, I was willing to take that chance with Gino. I felt I had nothing to lose considering where I was in life already. I had no dreams or ambitions. I was too busy trying to exist in everyday life; I had no Idea where I was going.

Everything was going well; we both called it quits at the restaurant because I was getting close to my labor date. I asked Titus to give Gino a job at his store so Gino would be close by when it was time for me to go into labor. Titus owned the liquor store for years so of course he was well known to the neighborhood, which is another reason I screwed around with the Chaldean a ways down versus with Titus. I knew not to ask the Chaldean I had previous dealings with to give Gino a job; that would've been scandalous, and a time-bomb waiting to explode.

I didn't put Gino's name on the lease; that way if he ever put his hands on me again, I could easily put him out.

Gino was there every step of the way during the entire pregnancy. He never missed a doctor's appointment, we were getting along great, but still, I wasn't in love.

When Raheem and Keevon were born and released from the hospital, Diane came down to the house to see them, and to also make a few phone calls, because her phone was disconnected as usual. It didn't take long before the Demon came out of Diane. There she started with the sarcastic subliminal remarks, trying to get under Gino's skin. She blamed him for my moving out and started name calling as she held the receiver in her hand to place her call. It damn near killed her pockets when I moved out I guess. I was also her stress reliever, because whatever she went through emotionally I had to pay for it; she kept me miserable right along with her.

Gino respectfully asked her to leave, and there the time-bomb exploded. He reached for the phone, but Diane cracked him upside the head with it before he could snatch it out of her hands, and the rumbling began. I screamed for the both of them to stop while adamantly trying to reach for my three sons. Tidus happened to be standing outside the store and heard all the commotion, because we lived in the corner house. He and his partner ran over quickly and came inside headed straight for Gino, and his partner grabbed Diane. When the fight was over Gino made it clear that Diane was no longer welcome in our home. What a messed-up situation my kids had to experience, especially the twins. It was their first day home from the hospital.

Things never went back to normal. Three months after the twins were born, Gino started using me as his punching bag, and the police never did a darn thing. Gino talked down about America so bad and all the Americans in it. He began to show the rest of his true colors. Gino showed a side of him I never pictured, other than putting the hands to me, because I'd seen that side of him already. He was a lover of Iraq, and used to go on and on yapping that all Americans were stupid and we didn't know how to speak proper English. Gino tried convincing me to read the Holy Koran. I tried it out, because I thought if we were equally yoked spiritually, our relationship would get better, but my spirit couldn't agree with all that was written; I tried. Because I took no interest in Gino's beliefs, he said God didn't love people like me, and the Holy Bible was a white man's bible.

Not only did Gino beat me, but he rigged the TV where I couldn't tune into anything. He took the speaker wires and telephone cords to work with him everyday so I would be left sitting at home with nothing. Gino did this every day! Our front and side door had inside deadbolt locks, and he started locking me and the kids in the house until he came home from work; all of the windows had security bars.

Gino could see the entire house from behind the counter at work. I feared him, especially when he threatened to take the twins back to the West Indies if I left him. He was good for slapping my business in my face and to other people. He ridiculed Diane's suicide attempts, and her getting psychological therapy. He said: *"If you even think of moving back with Diane, I'll tell the courts everything about her crazy a**, and they'll take the kids from you, because her home is an unstable living environment."*

I didn't want to take any chances on moving back in with her. I definitely didn't want to go back to that life. I wasn't working anymore and Gino stopped helping me financially; everything was jacked up. I felt like I had no way out. He was running my life, the house, and only paying the phone bill; the phone that I could not use. Gino only provided for the boys, not me. Not only did I severely regret hooking up with him, but I hated myself for hooking him up with the job at the store.

Gino had a habit of spitting on me after beating me. Once I was beat-down to the ground he would kick me dead in the pit of my stomach. He drenched my face with beer every time I called the police, and then tell them I started the fight because I was drunk. The same two white officers came out every time. I begged them to smell my breath, but all they did was laugh at me and walk back to their squad cars. The police told me if I called them again, they were taking me to jail. As usual, Gino escorted them back to their squad car, ridiculing Diane and me like we were animals, and they'd all laugh hilariously. I can't judge if they were prejudiced or not; maybe it was Gino's nationality that fascinated them. I felt I had no place in the world; I was just an existence. I didn't know what to do or how to think. I only knew how to give and love.

I used to stand at the foot of our bed when Gino was sleeping, watching him with a dark, blank look. Thinking about the first time he'd put his hands on me and how our relationship had gone volatile. I wanted to kill Gino; set him on fire. I thought that was my only way of winning. He was much stronger than I was. Diane didn't care and the cops didn't either. Every time I stood over Gino, I heard a whisper, *"Kill him."* I was full of resentment and regret. I knew if I killed him I was headed up state, and the twins would end up in the State's custody. It's so sad to not even know if Diane would've taken the twins under her care or not, or if the state would've even allowed her to keep them, listening to Gino. I just continued to take my life day by day, not having hope for what tomorrow may have brought.

I took the boys to see Diane and Uncle Damon. Gino didn't want the twins visiting with her, but every now and then I found a way to get him to allow them to visit with her rather she wanted to see them or not. I waited until he was in a good mood, which was very rare. While there, Diane never spoke to me or displayed any love to the twins. She didn't even look at us; her attention was on Daevon only so I grabbed the twins and we left.

Gino and I ran into my neighbor Mona in the hallway. She was an older lady who lived upstairs from us, and a friend of Diane's. I was headed to the basement to do laundry while the boys were napping when Mona said: *"Are you all right?"*

"I know you've heard all of the commotion that's been going on," I said.

Gino let out a fake laugh, playing it off. *"She crazy—she's the one who starts it all."*

"She don't believe that because she lives right over us and she can hear everything, and not to mention I'm sure Diane has told her a lot," I said.

Mona reached down in her jean pocket and pulled out a

business card and gave it to me; "psychiatric therapy" was printed on the front. That didn't surprise me. I already had intuition
that she and Gino were screwing around. I never accused them
or bothered asking just to be lied to or get beat by Gino. I gave
Mona her card back, which obviously she needed most, because
it was in her possession in the first place. I went on and continued my laundry leaving her and Gino standing in the hallway.

I was fed up with Gino. How stupid could I have been? I
got involved with someone I wasn't in love with, and the way
he was beating on me was obvious that he wasn't in love either.
I hated him, especially when he said he was glad Daevon wasn't
his son because of his light skin. Gino hated light-skinned
blacks. He was mentally messed up, right along with Mona.
She should've hooked Gino up with her personal shrink.

I packed Daevon's things, because I didn't want him to hear
the nasty comments that came from Gino. I let him spend a
couple weeks with Diane. I knew she'd love that considering how
many times she begged me to let her have him, which I absolutely
would not do; he spent enough time with her. Every time Gino
threatened to beat me I would send Daevon down the street with
Diane because I didn't want him around that either. He waited
until the twins were sleeping; Gino didn't want his own seeds to
see the monster he truly was. I had nowhere to send them, not
that Gino would have let me anyway, but I didn't want them in
the midst of chaos either and potentially end up traumatized in
life like I was. I had to make some moves, I had no idea how, but
I had to face my fears somehow, someway.

One morning Keevon woke up whining; he was the aggres-
sive twin. I knew it was feeding time, so I went into the kitchen
to prepare breakfast. All of a sudden Keevon screamed like he
never had before! I never heard him scream that way. I hurried
into the room and Gino was just standing there with a sinister

look on his face. I asked, *"What's wrong with him? Why is he crying like that?"* My spirit lead me to believe Gino pinched him. Gino smacked the taste out of my mouth right in front of Keevon and Raheem. I saw a two-by-four with nails sticking out lying up high across the window seal. I grabbed it with all intentions of killing Gino. He snatched it before I could get a good grip on it and knocked me down to the floor, and told me not to talk back to him, and then took off for work.

I was so tired of Gino boxing me like I was his opponent in the ring. I wasn't strong enough to fight back. I had no one to reach out to. My uncle Damon didn't care, because he and Diane were two peas in a pod.

As soon as Gino left for work I walked over to the foot of the bed, and I kneeled down to my knees and prayed. Praying was my only option. There was no way that I was going to accept God loving Gino and not me: *"Father, Gino said you don't love me. How can that be? But you love a person who abuses their children and the mother who conceived them? Father, if you can hear me and you love me, please lift me Lord. Remove me away from this relationship once and for all and I will never look back or turn my back on you."* I wasn't familiar with the term *"in Jesus' name"*, but the words rolled off my tongue so naturally.

Diane thought Gino was in the garage working out, which is what he usually did after work or on his day off. She made a homemade cocktail and tried to blow Gino to hell, but he wasn't in there; I guess she cared after all. I never admitted to Gino that Diane did it.

Gino jumped on me one last time. I mean we fought like Mike Tyson and Evander Holyfield. We swung at each other one last time, and landed a punch at the same time; he busted my lip, and I closed his right eye. That was the second and the last time the twins saw their parents fighting; Gino took off and went to work. Nina and her sister stopped by and for once, I wasn't locked in. I had my back faced them as I told them to come in. I didn't want them to see my swollen lip; thank God they'd only stopped by for a moment. One time Nina was over visiting and Gino and I were into it, because he accused me of drinking one of his beers when I didn't. Nina was just laughing hilariously! I didn't think anything was funny considering the life I was living. I had no one to turn to! I was literally jacked up in life; I absolutely could not turn to Nina!

I couldn't believe it! Princeton finally came to visit Diane, he and all six of his nephews. His oldest nephew Ron came down the street, knocking on my door. Ron was someone I kicked it with during Diane and Princeton's relationship. The twins were in their playpen, looking out of the picture window. As soon as Gino opened the door, the other five nephews came from no-where and rushed Gino; this was two days later after Gino and I had our last fight. I tried breaking it up, because Keevon and Raheem were right there watching everything. I was raised in a violent household all through my childhood, and it used to scare the daylights out of me. I definitely didn't want my sons around that environment any more than they already were.

There were things being thrown toward Gino, and through my picture window. Thank God the window had a double layer of glass. I didn't know who was throwing what—I was trapped in the hallway, unable to get hold of the twins. By the time I saw anything Gino ducked, and a 40 oz Old English beer bottle came flying straight towards my head and cracked it open to the white meat. Blood covered the white walls in the hallway and drenched my entire face and the top half of my body. I tried my best to break the fighting up. I didn't want it to travel in the front room, where the twins were. Even after get-ting my head smashed, the fight continued on. I had no choice, but to stagger out the side door in hopes of seeing Princeton to stop his nephews, because of the twins being in the midst of it all. I saw a blurred vision of Diane standing across the street in safety, holding on to the hands of Daevon and Princeton's daughter, laughing her heart out. She didn't have a care in the world about the twins' safety. Drenched in blood, I screamed for everybody to stop. "THE TWINS ARE IN THE FRONT ROOM. STOP, STOP, STOP!" No one listened. When Diane saw me drenched in blood, her laugh turned upside down, and she started to panic! When she yelled stop, they all listened.

I was rushed to the hospital. As I lay there getting thirteen stitches externally and internally, I thought about the irrational decision I made allowing Gino in my life. I was just trying to get away from Diane and find my own way. I had good intentions, but unfortunately I went about it the wrong way.

When I was released from the hospital and arrived home, Gino had a house full of people, including Diane's next-door neighbor, selling any and everything he could in the house. Gino bought it all and he sold it all. He took the money, and purchased a one-way plane ticket to Ft. Lauderdale, Florida. Gino left us with one sofa, a bed, and peace of mind, and that was all we needed.

God loved me after all. I had my sons, our life, and our freedom, and nothing was more important than that. It had only been forty-eight hours since I kneeled to my Father for help. From that day forward I began to know Jesus. I forgave Gino and continued to live my life.

> *I want you to have victory over the*
> *very thing that broke you, instead of*
> *being a victim of it.*
> *Iyanla Vanzant*

7

Motherless Child

My stepsister Carmen started coming by more often. She and her mother had everyday drama like any other mother and child, but their relationship was normal compared to mine and Diane's.

I allowed Carmen to move in with me as she was my only sister. We invited our friends over and just partied; for the first time I was doing me. I needed laughter in my life after being in bondage for nearly a year. I started job hunting at least two days a week, and two Fridays out of the month I hung out at the motorcycle clubs. You'd think, being saved through the grace of God from an abusive relationship, that I'd attend church on Sundays. I actually never thought about that. The most I did was read Bible stories to my sons and pray with them.

When Carmen moved in, our dad started coming over. I guess she was our bridge to a brand-new beginning. I loved my daddy very much, but unfortunately I didn't know him like I used to due to the years that gapped between us thanks to Diane. Carmen noticed I didn't call him Daddy and it saddened her. But the word "Daddy" didn't roll off my tongue naturally like "in the name of Jesus" did. I tried rehearsing it before he came to visit, but it wasn't working for me. He actually gave me my first Bible and gave me specific scriptures to read. I read bit by bit, and before I knew it I was calling him Daddy without even realizing it was coming out of my mouth.

I paid Nina's sister Lashana to watch after the twins on the weekends that I hung out at the motorcycle clubs, but that didn't last long at all. One morning Nina called and said, *"Come and getcha' kids because they being mistreated,"* and then I heard laughter in the background.

Twice I noticed when picking the twins up from their house, I'd walk in and everyone was downstairs eating breakfast or playing with the other kids, all except my mines. Every voice would silence when I entered the house. The twins were the only ones sitting at the top of the stairs, all alone with heavily soiled Pampers from piss and poop and swollen eyes from crying. Lashana would say, *"I was just getting ready to change them."* I'd glance at everyone, because they all had sinister smiles on their faces. I didn't believe Lashana; if she didn't want to be bothered with my sons, she should've said something. I could tell before I came over I was the topic of the conversation and it was all negative. I never took my twins over there again. From that point on I backed away from going around them so much, but kept hoping my relationship with them would change. Why? Again, I don't know.

I was tired of being talked about and mistreated year after year after year. I hated them for that. I would've never mistreated their children. I blamed myself. I chose to be involved with that family; they didn't choose me!

Diane wanted me to move back in with her, because as usual she was falling short on her mortgage, and still, I didn't want to take her up on the offer. I couldn't picture myself re-living that drama all over again, especially after all I had gone through. She bragged about how much money I would save if we shared the bills, but I knew how it would turn out in the end. I had more peace struggling to raise my sons in our own home than living in chaos in someone else's.

Tuesday afternoon Diane asked if Daevon could visit. She never asked about the twins, but that didn't stop me from allow-ing her to see Daevon whenever she wanted. It was the end of the month, and I was cooking a pot of stew to last us for the next few days. I still hadn't messed around with the Chaldean, and Carmen was still in high school. She didn't have a job. Although my dad and I were at a fresh start, I didn't ask him for money; I still didn't know how to reach out to him. I asked Diane for a few dollars, but she claimed she didn't have it; she had it.

Carmen's friends were visiting when Protective Services came knocking on my door at 7 p.m. that same Tuesday eve-ning *"We need to talk to you."* Someone had called anonymous-ly, indicating that I abused my children, locked them in their rooms, and wasn't feeding them. They walked through my home, checked the doorknobs, made me strip my twins naked, and went all through my fridge and kitchen cupboards. They inquired about a bruise over Daevon's eye; I was startled, be-cause he was in perfect condition when he left to go to Diane's, as always. Everyone started looking at each other in confusion. It would've been obvious if there was a bruise over my son's eye, especially with his light skin, and I'm sure Diane would've noticed it earlier when I walked him up the street to her house.

"Daevon didn't have any bruises when he left here earlier," I said.

After thoroughly observing the twins and our living condi-tions, the social worker didn't feel the need to remove the kids from the home.

I was asked to take a two-week parenting class specifically preparing me to plan a budget on a month-to-month basis. They set up one more follow-up appointment to come out and check my kitchen for a food stock. They didn't get too deep into my business with the twenty-one questions; their concern was budgeting and keeping food on the table. Protective services told me that Diane was the one who called; they said she only wanted custody of Daevon and not the twins. I told them she asked me a few times in the past if she could have custody of him, but I told her no. This was the other reason they didn't bother building a case against me, because they couldn't understand if I was such a bad mother, why would Diane only want custody of, but one child.

I strolled down the street to check Daevon's eye and to tell Diane what just happened. There was no way I could have believed Diane would do something that dirty to any of her grandchildren, but her favorite grandchild? No way! Plus, blame me? No way! In the midst of explaining to Diane what happened when Protective services came out, I turned my attention to Daevon and I noticed a bruise over his left eye. I was flabbergasted! *"WHAT HAPPENED TO HIM?"*

Diane stuttered for a few seconds before saying, *"He had that when you brought him here earlier."*

"Mama, Daevon didn't have any bruises on him. Why would you do something like this?"

She continued on nervously and trying to blame Mona, my upstairs neighbor. I was baffled: *Why would Diane do this? Why was I such a dumb, blind, naïve, and gullible chick?* Protective Services put two and two together before I did, and Diane being my mother was all the more reason I should've known her better than they did. Eventually, it all made sense. Diane was paying me back for not wanting to move back in with her.

Diane was dangerously vindictive. She had a habit of doing things out of spite. I don't know if Diane used makeup to make Daevon's eye look bruised or if it really was bruised. I never touched it, because I didn't want to cause him any additional pain. I only looked at it. I just couldn't wrap my mind around thinking that Diane would do something so horrific. On the other hand, I could see her conspiring to do what she had to do to get custody of Daevon, potentially using makeup to create the illusion of a bruise. I just didn't know. I may have been in denial with the make-up excuse I don't know. I just couldn't see Diane doing such a horrific thing like that to her first beloved grandson.

Out of all people I called Nina's mother. I was in dismay and felt like my back was against the wall, with no other options. Instead of asking Diane for money again to buy food, I asked Nina's mother for some canned goods, something she always kept in stock. I was going to give it all back as soon as Protective serves left my house, because I didn't really need it. Although I had enough food to carry us over for a few days, I didn't trust Protective Services. I didn't trust anyone for that matter. I just needed to be on top of my game! My fear was not having enough for Protective Services' standards. The entire situation was surprisingly shocking to me coming from Diane and all. It happened so suddenly. I didn't want to take any chances.

Nina's mother said she would have one of her kids bring them by later. The next day had come and gone and still no canned goods. I called and asked what happened, and she said, *"I can't do it. I'm low on canned food."* Deep down in my spirit I felt that wasn't the truth or she wouldn't have offered it in the first place. If I remember correctly, all the years I had known them canned goods were something she never ran out of. The older I became the more Nina's mother couldn't stand me. There were lots of issues I had experienced through the years with the family that deeply wounded me emotionally and mentally, but OK! I packed those snake-biting-situations in the can and placed it right next to all the other cans stored in my head mentally. All I did was suck up to Nina's mom, because I wanted her to love me like a daughter. I was always looking for some form of motherly love. I didn't know what a mother's love felt like after T'mone came into Diane's life. I remember the first time I decided to open up to Nina's mother about me being raped, and her exact words were: *"Oh, girl, no wonder you crazy!"* She and her children fell out laughing as I froze up in embarrassment. I quote: I'll never forget that day. I was a fool for telling her. I should've kept it canned up like I had done all those years.

Anyway, God made sure I had more than enough food that I had no room to stock it all!

I separated myself from any affiliations with Diane. I lived my life and she lived hers; the only communication we had was when it was concerning Daevon. Nothing and no one affected me emotionally and mentally the way Diane did, because she was my everything. She was my mother and I loved her with everything I had!

Sometimes when I stepped outside to grab the mail, Diane would walk past my house holding Daevon's hand looking straight ahead. She wouldn't utter a word to me or the twins, but I kept my head up.

Lying on the grass under the mailbox was a dirty, wrinkled letter that looked like it had been run over by a car. The letter was from Wayne County Friend of the Court. Daevon had been removed from my custody and placed with Diane from right up under my nose! The court date was postdated two days prior to me receiving it. Diane did it again!

I notified the court and explained to them how I had literally just found the letter lying on the grass underneath my mailbox. It was all too late; they annotated my rights step by step on how to fight my case. I didn't know how to fight against Diane. I knew how powerful Diane was and knew I would lose, because she had a Dirty-D-Doctorates'-Degree.

Daevon was cut off from my benefits, because Diane applied for welfare assistance and Social Security for him, but was ineligible because of her income. She felt that Daevon needed speech therapy which is why she applied for the SSI, but he was denied. I continued providing entirely for my son's needs. Diane went through hoops to bring me down, all because I wouldn't move in with her. She left me clueless and destitute, conniving her way in the system to get custody of Daevon. Although it was unfortunate conceiving more children out of wedlock, I was so grateful having the twins by my side, loving me unconditionally since I'd halfway lost Daevon.

A year had gone by when Diane decided to start speaking again. She approached me again about moving in to help her with the bills. I hated to revert back to a jacked-up situation, but my enervation caused me to give in. I loved Diane so much, so I kept pressing on, and trying, hoping that we could become mother and daughter again. We hadn't been since I was fifteen, and I was now twenty-two. I let my house go and Carmen moved back with her mother.

I needed so desperately to be close to Diane, but every time I got too close she'd snake-bite me and it would sting even worse than before. Diane knew exactly how and where to bite me. She knew what she was doing and she did it well; I was naïve and gullible. I didn't understand. She had a scandalous, vindictive, and manipulative personality, especially when it came to me. She knew when things got rough, I would run to her for refuge and comfort, and she could swiftly string me like Pinocchio.

Diane allowed our neighbor Debbie to move in with us as well, because she was having some financial difficulties. She must have been paying Diane good money for room and board because I didn't have to pay any rent…wow! What was the catch? This wasn't like Diane!

My room was in the basement, just enough room for me and the twins. The basement was finished, it even had a fireplace and of course a bathroom. I started saving what I could as soon as possible; I knew that Diane was bound to flip the script at any given moment. I followed her request in allowing her to put away my savings so I wouldn't dip into them. I guess this was my way of trying to establish a mother and daughter relationship as usual. I wasn't all that comfortable because I knew she had a bad disposition, but I went along with it anyway.

I was dreaming I was in a white florescent room with a man dressed in a brown suit sitting on a brown bench. I walked up to the man, and he said: *"I am going to clear you of blindness so that you may see what's going on around you."* I woke up to the gospel song "God Is Trying to Tell You Something." I cried a river of tears. For the first time in my life…I felt God throughout my entire body; the Holy Spirit! I never felt that way; it felt so good. I felt genuinely loved; it felt so authentic, like nothing I'd ever felt before. It felt like a spiritual orgasm; WOW! I could not stop crying even if I was slapped across the face. God was all over me; lol, I couldn't shake'm even if I wanted to! I was singing Salt-N-Pepa's lyrics: Whatta' Man Whatta' Man Whatta Mighty Good Man! I could feel Him!

I began to see Diane's character more clearly, and in a different light; I guess that's why the room in my dream was

florescent, other than my being in a Holy atmospere. She talked about me to her friends like I was nobody, and I sat in my
room listening while tears drenched my face, and rolled down
to my pillow.

She and Debbie depended on me to do most of the cooking. Debbie had one grandchild who visited on a regular basis,
and Diane had Daevon. Since I had the twins and Daevon was
biologically my child, I was to do most of the cooking; I didn't
mind. I guess this time I didn't whip up dinner fast enough so
Diane and Debbie left with both the grandkids, and left the
twins.

A half hour later they came walking through the kitchen. I
saw their eyes widen because the twins were sitting at the table
eating a three-course meal. I knew they were going to buy the
other kids burgers or pizza and weren't going to bring anything
back for the twins. It was something they did on a regular basis,
so I whipped up a quick meal. I didn't want the twins feeling
left out. I didn't want to see them saddened. I did everything in
my power to protect their feelings. I knew what it felt like to be
left out when Diane and Darren were married. I used to tell her
about that, but she never did anything, so I became receptive to
it. I fought hard not to let it get the best of me, because I knew
nothing was gonna change; I had grown to accept rejection.
What I wasn't going to do was allow the twins to be subjected
to it. I was going to make sure they grew up strong, mentally
and emotionally stable; not stupid like I felt I was.

When Daevon and Debbie's grandchild came walking in
with burgers, fries, and milkshakes, the twins didn't budge or
cut one eye at them. One day we would be first, and all who
mistreated us would be last; someday we would shine...some
day!

I was relaxing one afternoon when I decided to flip the

script for a change. I called Diane to the basement and asked her for my savings. I decided to go to a shelter. Diane told me I owed her that money because the kids had stopped up her toilet and she needed a plumber. All of the children played in the basement because that was the play area; I had no privacy. I felt it would've been fair if all three adults split the cost of plumbing expenses. However, it didn't go that way. I was the unfortunate one. She gave me bus fare for one way and sent me on my way, broke.

> *I don't care what you lose, hold*
> *on to your integrity; you are who*
> *you are.*
> *Bishop T.D. Jakes*

8

Existing in Limbo

The shelter held twenty-five cots that lay side by side, and no lockers or dressers; all belongings were to be slid under the bed. Lights out by 10 p.m. and by morning everyone was up at 5:00 sharp to be out by 7:00, and if you weren't back by 5 p.m. you lost your cot. With all the rules and regulations, I still had more peace there than what I had when living with Diane. I resided in the shelter for three months until Carmen told her mother where I was. Sheila called my dad immediately and asked him to come get me, and bring me over there with her and Carmen. I was reluctant to go, because it was my life and my problem; that's why I never told my dad.

Sheila told Carmen and me that her house was in foreclosure, so she was moving back south, and we could stay there at least six months and save money. Carmen's best friend, Arielle, came by to visit and she heard the news, and then she wanted to move in. There were four bedrooms, so it was enough space; it was a blessing from God to live six months rent-free.

Carmen had a son and named him Marlon, and Arielle was

pregnant with her first child. She and I were never close; she was always in competition with me for some reason. I couldn't understand what she was competing with. Arielle had a good man who provided for her, and fine as he wanted to be. He took good care of her. Every time the two of them hung out, they wore matching outfits and shoes; that was too cute. Me, I had three kids with deadbeat daddies and no real man in my life, so I didn't know what her problem was. I should've been the one jealous.

Arielle had a baby girl. I had never seen a baby so beautiful in all my life. Her baby's skin was dark chocolate smooth, and creamy with thick, jet-black curly hair, and had cheeks like Tweety Bird's grandmother. Arielle named her baby Shilice. Carmen and Arielle were good mothers, but it didn't stop them from hittin' them streets. They knew how much I loved those babies, so instead of asking me to babysit they'd just tell me they would be back, and out the front door they went.

Six months was right around the corner, and Carmen found her place before any of us. Sheila drove in town and snuck up on us on a Sunday morning, because she knew how we partied on the weekends. When she turned the key to come in, the smell of alcohol slapped her across the face, and the house was a total wreck.

She was ready to close the house up since Carmen had found her a new place. Finding a place for me was challenging until Diane called. She was moving out, and was in need of me renting her house, so I thought maybe I could work with that as long as she wasn't living there—that would be something new. I also had to take into consideration that I had no time to buy, our six months was just about up.

Carmen's plans however, backfired and she ended up not getting the house she found. Sheila told me, *"Carmen is still your sister, so look out for her.*" I looked at her like she was crazy and thought, *It sure is funny how the tables turn. God don't like ugly.* Sheila took me in from the shelter and I appreciated that, but I also took Carmen in back in the day too. Here we still had five weeks left to find a place, and she was ready to close house as soon as she thought Carmen had herself together. She didn't take into consideration that I stood a chance of going back to a shelter with my twins.

With time not being in my favor, I had no choice but to take up Diane's offer without even thinking it through. Sheila also had no choice but to wait before closing the house up, because Carmen was still house hunting until I told Diane to let her move in too. I had no intentions of turning my back on Carmen.

Eventually Arielle and her baby daddy moved in, and so did Gary. I had known him since he was fifteen. I used to hang out with his brother, and as the years went by, Gary and I became close friends.

We all went out on New Year's Eve, something I never did. We had just come from one club and were headed to an after-hours joint. My spirit led me not to go because we were headed for a bad accident. I didn't sense anything until we were halfway to our destination, so I took it as too late to go back. I tried to fight the feeling and prayed for protection, but the more I prayed and tried to let it go, the more intense the feeling became. I told everybody what I was feeling and told Gary to take us home. Everybody got mad. *"Girl, ain't nothin' gone happen; stop sayin' that. You thinkin' negative."* They just wanted to go out, they were young and into the streets; I know what the Holy Spirit was telling me.

We were at a red light and the car mysteriously stalled. Gary got out and popped the hood; he figured it was the engine belt, because it was squeaking loudly as it spun around the pulley. He snatched it off, talking about we didn't need it. Of course we needed it! I began making my way out of the car and told everybody else to get out so we could push the car to the curbside and get it out of the middle of the street. Gary was still standing there trying to figure out what to do, high as hell. The girls didn't want to get out. Carmen was pregnant with her second child, and her friend that tagged along with us was seven months pregnant.

EERRRG! BOOM! A minivan was speeding up the commercial street, traveling every bit of sixty miles per hour. I tried running across the street before he slammed into us, but my foot was tangled up in the seat belt so I never had the chance to get completely out of the car. Gary stood in front of me, trying to push me back in, in hopes of saving my life, but it was all too late. The van hit Gary, who flew eight feet into the air, and then crashed down onto the driver's windshield. We had been hit so hard by the minivan that it pushed our car across the red light, straight to the other side of the street. Everything began moving in slow motion, as in a movie. I was being dragged on the ground with my right hand on the bottom of the steering wheel and my left hand on the door handle; my foot still stuck. I saw glass and gas flying everywhere, and I then looked down as I watched my butt and legs being dragged across the ground. It was a moment in a trance; everything went silent and in slow motion like a near death experience. When it all came to a stop, I didn't know if I was dead or alive.

Thank God for hearing my prayers, because every one of us came out with only minor injuries. The guy who hit us was drunk and he had the nerve to get out of the van, trying to beat Gary with a baseball bat. The cops restrained him and took him to jail. When Diane saw that I was fine from the accident, she ordered me to replace her sweat suit I borrowed for the night; she was something else!

We all sued except Carmen's pregnant friend, who definitely should have sued. She ended up having a breech delivery, but the baby was healthy, thank God!

Renting from Diane lasted a year; it basically ran its course. I believe God had it set up that way, because I had come to find out Diane wanted to rent the house out to someone else. Also everybody was scared of T'mone's apparitions. I always heard the same story from different people who rented the house. Renters complained about furniture moving upstairs in the bedrooms when no one was up there or dishes flying across the kitchen, crashing to the floor and breaking. I even heard stories of him walking in the walls, and then he would fly out and quickly disappear into the fireplace, but only if there was firewood burning. He rattled doorknobs violently if you were in the room. Arielle and Carmen hated when I left them home alone. They felt safe when I was there, because I wasn't scared of him, T'Mone was scared of me; there is power in the name of Jesus.

Surprisingly Diane had enough courtesy to give us a couple of months to find a place to live. Her intentions were to rent the house out to a lady and her kids, and charge her the same monthly amount she was charging me. Diane had a beautiful brick house. It was a colonial style home with not one fireplace, but two, and the neighborhood was up to part. She had the prettiest and largest house on the block. The lady who wanted to rent it owned a fashion store outlet and was doing quite well for herself, and she and her kids were earning even more money by selling clothes at home too. I couldn't understand why Diane was only charging her three hundred.

I was still living in the house when Carmen and the others moved out. Diane started bringing the lady to the house, discussing business and giving tours throughout the house. I mean she brought her all upstairs where my private domain was; that was inconsiderate and disrespectful.

Every time that lady came over, the smell of her butt and vagina peeled the flesh off my face; my nose was trying to run away without me. Please don't get me wrong, I had no problem with Diane renting the house, but don't invade my privacy viewing the property while I was still residing there paying rent. And at least get some bread for it. She was selling herself short. I really didn't see the point, because three hundred was what we were paying monthly. Diane's house was worth every bit of eight hundred dollars a month, and this was back in the early 90's.

I moved in with my dad for six weeks while working midnights to save up for another place to live. He didn't mind keeping an eye on the twins because they slept all through the night. He took me to work at night and picked me up at 7 a.m., because buses didn't run that route, but then he had to rush to work. Every morning when I got in from work, I prepared breakfast for Keevon and Raheem, and we watched *Sesame Street* and *Barney*. We sang the famous "I Love You" Barney song, but after that I always started to nod off. I stressed the issue to the boys to please stay in the room and watch videotapes, play with the toys, or read. I spent a lot of quality time with them; they knew their ABCs and how to count to twenty at eleven months, and they were potty-trained before they were thirteen months and reading at three years old.

I lived off what I earned at the job and saved my welfare checks; in six weeks we moved to a two-bedroom complex. I wasn't able to work the job anymore because I nodded off one morning, and when I woke up the twins were outside alone. I have no idea how they could have unlocked the side door, but they did; it was obvious the midnight shift wasn't going to work out anymore. Also, it was too much on my dad driving me back and forth, and then having to rush out for work himself so I let the job go.

I loved my new place. It was newly remodeled. It was peaceful—so peaceful that I began to feel very lonely. I sat in the middle of the floor and thought about my past life experiences. Diane was still the same. I still hadn't overcome my childhood maltreatment. My self-esteem had hit rock bottom. I was lost, lonely, and felt unloved, believing that my sons and I had nothing to live for. I had no expectations in life, no drive or ambition. I only knew how to live by the day. It was like riding on a merry-go-round; every time the ride was over, I got off at the same exact spot I first started. I was just existing in limbo; I needed to free myself, live, and enjoy life to it's fullest. I just didn't know how to.

I kneeled to my knees, and began crying out for God to come take me and the twins' life. I pictured walking us out into the Bell Isle River and drowning us, but thought that would be selfish to my boys, not giving them a fair chance in life. I didn't know where I was going, didn't know what I wanted, because I had no ambition. I just wanted to go back in essence with God, and take my twins with me. I didn't want to leave them living in the cold world in the care of unloving hands; no one loved them like me. Daevon was all right. He had Diane, and he was all she cared about.

A couple of weeks later I barked up on a job through my uncle Damon. I took the Sempta Transportation there and back. As much as I didn't want to depend on Diane to babysit, I had no other options. I had more bills to pay, plus the job came about so fast I had to leap out on faith and go for it; I literally started working the first day I applied for the position. I had to make a living for my family. God didn't see fit for our lives to end. He wanted me to get over it, stay strong, and keep it moving, to where? I didn't know, I just kept pressing on.

9

Flown From The Cuckoo's Nest

I was riding the bus to work when a guy walked up the isle and introduced himself as Darnell; he said he'd been watching me for a while. I was interested in knowing how long a while was, considering all the eccentric weirdoes that lived in the world. I hadn't been in a relationship since Gino, I had become more cautious.

Every day of the week Darnell and I rode together to work and ate together during lunch break. Darnell had become my comforter; he was very attentive to me, and cared about my every thought and mood. He never came on too strong or undressed me with his eyes; he treated me with respect. I talked to him about my unstable relationship with Diane, that's how comfortable I was around him. It was so easy talking to him that I didn't even notice all the things that rolled off my tongue regarding my life's history. In the midst of telling him how money hungry Diane was, he reached down in his pocket and pulled out three hundred dollars without thinking twice. I wasn't used to a real man; Darnell was a real man.

Diane, on the other hand, didn't like him, and it killed her to know that someone loved and provided for me. Darnell was a threshold in my life. Diane didn't like that; she wanted me to be dependent upon her for any and everything. She loved power and control, at least over me.

When I worked overtime, Diane picked me up from the bus terminal once I arrived in the city. Sometimes Darnell would be sitting outside my doorstep when I pulled up, hoping I wouldn't be upset by his dropping by unannounced. Diane used to look at him like he was crazy, wondering what the heck he was doing in front of my yard. When I invited him over after work, he rode with me and Diane, which was usually payday. Diane had her hand out for babysitting, gas money, and anything else she pencil-whooped me for. I didn't have a problem with paying what I owed, but once she placed that pencil in between her thumb and index finger, I ended up owing her almost triple the amount. Diane added up things she accused me of owing her way back when I was fifteen or sixteen years old. When she ran out of pencil lead, I ended up owing her my entire check. As usual she had the nerve to ask if I needed to borrow money; her way of keeping me in debt and dependent upon her. She was draining me.

Darnell was fed up. He gave me a signal to tell Diane no, and I trusted him. From that day forward I never had to ask Diane for another dime. Diane didn't like that, at all!

Diane made me suffer terribly. Every morning, I was forced to get up a few hours early to walk the twins almost two miles to school in dead midwinter, and then make it back in time to catch the bus for work. The snow was three to four inches deep when we walked the twins to school and they were only four years old. I truly appreciated Darnell coming by in the mornings to walk with us or sometimes take a taxi. It hurt me to the core of my heart watching the twins as they looked into Diane's van with Daevon sitting all warm and cozy. I was even more hurt to look at Daevon as he watched us walk by and didn't even speak to us. I knew Diane's making a difference between the siblings was going to cause drama and division among them in the future.

I invited Darnell over one Sunday for dinner; I thought it was time for him to really get to know the boys other than when we walked them to school. I cooked collard greens, macaroni and cheese, candied yams, smoked turkey, neck bones, and buttermilk cornbread. Darnell never went home again.

He told me he was living in a halfway house from being incarcerated due to aggravated assault on a guy who owed him money. Upon his release, he finally told me he was staying with an associate in need of a place to stay or he wouldn't be released. That was one of his perks I could appreciate, because he didn't come on strong, trying to use me. I mean here I had a man paying my rent when he didn't really have a pot to piss in for himself. Darnell had become an essential part of me and the kids life. He respected us, he catered to my every being; he treated me like I deserved to be treated, like a queen. Although I continued bouncing my head on my pillow, imagining living in another world to escape reality, I began holding my head up a little higher. I was beginning to feel comfortable with myself, my self-esteem was gradually leveling up. I actually started living, and hadn't even realized it. I was learning to love me. My self-consciousness, on the other hand, was a work in progress, but at least I was aware and revising.

Halloween season rolled around and Diane offered to buy the twins costumes and take them trick-or-treating, up until she got pissed off about something so petty that I can't even remember what it was. Instead of the treat we got tricked!

Darnell and I had to think of something quick for the twins' costume. They had Burger King crowns that came with their meals earlier on in the week. Darnell walked to the dollar store for food coloring, glue, cotton balls, face paint, and Magic Markers. We used the boys' two-piece white thermal sets, colored in large circles, decorated their crowns, and made clown hats.

We walked nearly two miles to the school, trying to make it in time for the Halloween party. The twins received first place prizes for best costumes; everybody took pictures, and the pictures were placed in the school's photo display. Diane even complimented them. Darnell and I were very proud, because we knew that halloween day would be a special memory for the twins.

Darnell and the twins and I walked neighborhood after neighborhood, getting their bags filled with treats. They had so much candy it was enough to carry them until the next Halloween season. Although I wasn't living right with the fornication and all, I truly appreciated God blessing us with Darnell. He was a genuine companion, someone who loved me unconditionally. Darnell was definitely a blessing to us.

Diane stopped by for a visit, in need of discussing her financial dilemmas. The stankin'-booty lady she rented her house to fell behind in payments. I didn't care if she was having financial problems; under no condition was I moving in with her. To my surprise, Diane didn't need a roommate. The problem was her being unable to buy Daevon anything for Christmas; as usual she didn't mention anything about gifts for Keevon and Raheem. Diane normally bought Daevon everything for Christmas and at least a gift or two for the twins. I started buying Daevon three or four gifts less than what I bought the twins so they'd all have the same number of gifts. I never once wanted Daevon to think the twins were more special than him just because they weren't all living together. I also didn't want the twins to see Daevon with more gifts than them. I refused to allow division among my children if I could help it.

Christmas morning all the boys were happy as usual, and Daevon had everything Diane had requested on her wish list.

Diane came by Christmas morning telling us she had gotten hold of some funds and was able to Christmas shop for Daevon after all. She packed up the gifts we bought him and took him home to a Christmas tree filled with gifts under it. Daevon had enough gifts for three kids; he had more gifts than he had room for. Diane played us again!

Daevon treated Darnell like he was irrelevant, and it all had to do with Diane talking negatively about him. I was already used to her talking about me and the twins to Daevon and everybody else. She told Daevon whenever he spent the night with us he didn't have to listen to Darnell, because he wasn't his daddy. She was just stirring up drama all over again in my relationship, but using Daevon to do it. Daevon talked back to Darnell and got his butt stung by Darnell. I allowed him to physically chastise Daevon. I knew all he needed was one butt whipping for him and Darnell to get an understanding and a connection just like Jody needed on "Baby Boy". I knew Darnell genuinely loved me and my children.

Darnell verbally chastised the twins one time, and they were crazy about him from there on. All the boys knew Darnell loved them, even Diane. I had three sons and not one of their dads was in the picture. Yes, a woman can raise a son to be respectful, have values, morals, and a strong upbringing spiritually. However, there are some things about manhood we will not understand, and vice versa. Therefore, boys tend to look to other male figures as their mentor because they understand one another, being of the same gender. Darnell and I had been going long and strong at least nine months. He was genuine, loving, and definitely a family man, and I trusted his parental guidance.

I dreamed the twins and I were living in a beautiful loft. We were sitting on the floor huddled together, because a tornado was hurtling over us. I held them in my arms securely as we watched the ceiling being snatched ruthlessly from over our heads and into the funnel of the tornado. The dream then skipped to me walking into a hospital room where Darnell lay there, sick.

I woke up feeling dizzy and nauseous from watching the roof spin rapidly in the tornado. I didn't know how to interpret the dream. Ever since the day I kneeled to God about Gino and made prayers an essential part of my life, I started having dreams; those dreams stuck with me.

Diane wanted the tenant out of her house asap! She was continuously behind on the rent. She was receiving negative reports from neighbors and the regular repairmen that rendered services on the house. Diane's house was infested with roaches, and continuous traffic ran in and out all through the night, disturbing the neighbors. Diane was tired of the negative reports, especially how the house had a bad odor of butt and vagina.

Diane had the nerve to ask me to be a witness in court. I was all in at first, but on the day of the court proceeding, she came knocking on my door, and I just lay there and thought about how she put me and the twins out for that broad and her kids, and for the same amount of rent. I didn't budge to open my door.

Two days later Diane came by with an attitude and I respectfully stood my ground for the first time. I was finally coming out of my shell.

I was pregnant with another son. Here I thought my morning sickness was from the tornado dream. I wasn't happy, because I was on daddy number three and still single; the crazy thing was, I wasn't ready to marry Darnell. Although he was a good man, father, and provider, I still wasn't sure if he was the guy I wanted to marry. Crazy, I know, right? Darnell and I were almost two years into the relationship, and still I needed more time. Anyway, Darnell was a proud man.

It was a cold February night when it rained heavily and flooded our place from back to front from sewerage backup. The carpet was soaked, and it filled the air with foulness. We drove to Diane's to spend the night until the landlord came out the next morning. We expected him to disinfect the premises by at least removing the carpet, but all he did was shampoo and dry it. We had him come back out, because we could still smell the odor heavily, but all he did was whine, saying there was nothing else he could do.

Diane insisted we all stay with her because she didn't want her grandsons living under a health hazard condition, and I was pregnant. I couldn't believe for once Diane never spoke a negative word about my being pregnant; good for herrr!

I called my dad to give him a heads-up on what was going on. I preferred moving in with him, but my dad didn't believe in playing house before marriage. He also knew moving in with Diane wasn't going to last. If things went sour, which more than likely they would, I trusted God to place it in my dad's heart to open up his doors to Darnell. My dad loved Darnell and knew he was a good man.

Diane and I had our usual warfare; I could tell she was about to change with the wind. Although I knew this was going to happen prior to moving in with her, I needed to take advantage of the opportunity. Even if it lasted two or three days, it gave Darnell and me time to put our heads together and figure out a plan.

However, it was time to go, and we weren't too adamant about having to continuously leave our kitten in the car in mid-winter. Diane hated pets and I understood that; her house, her rules. I went out to my car to grab a few shirts out of the suitcase in the backseat; I never unpacked the car because I knew it was temporary at Diane's crib. I noticed a huge dent on the back driver side; I mean it looked like it got smacked hard. The car was parked in front of the house, so how it ended up smashed on the on the back-side the way it was, was beyond me. I could understand if there were a driveway across the street and someone potentially backed into it speeding out, but that wasn't the case. It looked as if it was done intentionally. I believe Diane had something to do with it.

Two nights prior to our car damage, Diane called her friend over in need of a favor. She was mad at someone, but I couldn't quite make out whom. I overheard her telling her friend to smack somebody's car. Her friend owned an old-school truck and I mean old-school; it wasn't made of fiberglass, but all metal. Not thinking twice about the request Diane asked her friend, I noticed a few nights later our car had been hit. I asked Diane about it, and she acted as if she didn't know anything, but the sinister look in her eyes and demonic smile she tried hiding told me she was behind it all. Diane was good for holding grudges and being vindictive. She was still mad from the disagreement we had a few days earlier, so not only was I prepared to get kicked out at any given moment, but I expected her to do something vindictive as a grand-finale.

Diane couldn't be a supportive mother or grandmother for even a week. She did what was expected of her; she went from Dr. Jekyll to Ms. Hyde over a darn cooking pot, which was actually her cue to put me out. She put us out in the middle of February, and it was below zero. My dad picked us up and moved us in with him, including Darnell.

Darnell had been in contact with his family who lived in Florida. They always talked about Detroit being the devil city and Florida being full of peace and beauty and easy-to-obtain employment. So we considered it; we had nothing to lose. Our relationship was going really well, so we thought why not start fresh in a new state? I spoke with his cousin Belinda and she went on and on about all the beautiful homes that were vacant. The only one who told us not to move down there was Belinda's brother Carlos, because he said it was the number one drug state in the country. We didn't let that faze us; we were from Detroit! If you could survive in the "D" you could survive anywhere in the country. Darnell and I thought long and hard about relocating; it was a major step, but we were looking for change. We wired Belinda four hundred dollars for a down payment for the security deposit and we purchased four one-way plane tickets.

The day we were leaving, Diane came by crying her heart out, claiming she went to the doctor and found out she was sick and was told she didn't have long to live. I looked at her like she was crazy; for once, I didn't fall for her bull. I gave her the enduring forehead kiss and said, "I'll keep you in my prayers." She was startled. She thought stealing custody of Daevon gave her power over me. I never forgot Darnell's encouraging words: *"It's time for you to let go, explore, and be your own woman. Let your mother raise Daevon, God will give him back to us in due season. She took him; now let her raise him."*

Before I met Darnell, back when Diane had my cash benefits and food stamps decreased, I was still providing for all of Daevon's needs. I was taking what little benefits I was getting for Keevon and Raheem and splitting them three ways to provide for all three boys equally. I needed Daevon to know how much I loved him and that it wasn't my fault. However, I had to trust in God. I had to trust that God would show Daevon the truth once he was mature enough to understand.

Diane didn't think I would take such a big step in life, but she was wrong. Darnell taught me how to fly from the cuckoo's nest, and Diane hated him for that. She pulled him into the other room to keep me from hearing how she threatened to have him murdered if anything happened to me in Florida.

10

Green Vision, Brown Reality

Florida was beautiful; it was definitely a state designed for re-tirees. We assumed Darnell's family would be at the airport waiting to pick us up as agreed, but no. We waited over an hour; first impression wasn't impressive at all, as was our first greeting over the phone.

Mr. Matthews drove; he was Darnell's uncle and he was also a pastor. Belinda, who sat on the passenger side, was Mr. Matthews's daughter. The long ride was quiet. I guess his family said everything they had to say over the phone a month ago. I sat quietly and listened to the sound of tires riding on wet pavement as every vehicle passed us by. I also heard sticky noises behind me like the sound of masking tape being peeled. I turned around to look, but didn't see anything. I just assumed it was the tires roll-ing on the wet pavement, but it sounded like the noise was com-ing from inside the car. Darnell and his cousin Belinda laughed because I was looking everywhere around me. I was petrified!

I heard it again so I checked thoroughly all around me. I looked to the right and instantly I freaked out! I felt like Chris

Tucker on *Friday* when he was sitting in the chicken coop tweekin'.

It looked like a brown mouse lying sideways on the window seal watching me! I froze. I was in total disbelief. I screamed! I lost it! *"THERE'S A MOUSE IN THE CAR!"* The laughter got louder, especially when I took a second look and noticed it wasn't a mouse, but a palmetto. I took a third look, because I absolutely could not believe my eyes. I dropped my head sideways as if, I was on some serious drugs. I could not believe my eyes! I lost my freakin' mind! I was nine months pregnant, trying to open up the back door and jump out into ongoing traffic on the freeway. I didn't care about anybody in that car, not even my unborn child. My stomach was stuck between the twins as I tried so desperately to get out, but I couldn't stretch any further. Darnell and Belinda were still laughing hilariously, because when I opened the door, my face was hanging out while the rest of my body was stuck. Darnell grabbed me as I prepared myself to smack face-first into fifty-five-mph traffic. I thought people exaggerated about huge flying roaches down south. It was bigger than a mouse and had the nerve to have wings; that was way too much for me.

Mr. Matthews took his sweet time exiting the freeway with a sinister smirk planted on his face; they all thought it was funny. Once we exited the freeway we turned in to a service station, and I tried jumping out before the car came to a complete stop. I was still being laughed at. I walked quickly into the mart. I had no intentions of getting back in the car until that roach was gone. As I stood in line waiting to purchase my snacks, I watched Darnell as he struggled to get the roach out. By the time I headed back outside, I guess the palmetto had flown out of the car, because everyone was getting back inside.

As soon as we were good on the freeway, I started hearing

sticky noises again. I squeezed my eyes shut as I frantically prayed all the way to the Matthews house, with my toes curled up tightly.

The next morning I met Mrs. Matthews, and we talked cordially as she prepared a quick breakfast. She was all right. She came off to me as a hardworking family woman just existing in life and going through the motion; she wasn't happy at all. I called Daevon and let him know we made it safely and told him I loved him. I spoke with him for a minute; I wanted to make sure his mind was as content as it was when I talked to him the day of the move.

After breakfast Mrs. Matthews drove us to the boys' new school as they were able to start the same day. While we were chauffeured around the city trying to get settled, I marveled at the state's beauty. Some of the palmetto trees were clustered with coconuts. I caught a glimpse of all the grapevines that grew alongside the fenced yards.

We went to the Secretary of State and applied for our Florida State drivers' licenses because Mr. Matthews put a word in for me where he worked for a car rental company.

When we arrived back to the house, Carlos had the grill smoking with burgers big as Mondo's on *Good Burger*. They were thick, huge, and medium rare; according to him that's how they were supposed to be eaten. I loved medium-rare steaks, not burgers. Carlos was Mr. Matthews's son; he was a funny dude, he was the spitting image of Michael Clarke.

The next morning we had hopes of Mrs. Matthews taking us house hunting. She didn't and neither did we bother to ask, because we respected the fact that she may have been tired working a midnight job. That one tired day turned into weeks, and not only that, Belinda spent the four hundred dollars that we wired her for our security deposit. She had no intentions of finding us a house; not once did she mention looking at one house when she and Mr. Matthews picked us up from the airport. Now that was a conversation that we should've been discussing instead of a long dull ride to the house .

Darnell began getting frustrated. I had now gone into labor, and we were still living with his family. I decided it was best to go through delivery alone at the hospital, because it'd only been a week since Darnell started working his new job. He didn't like the thought of it, but we had to do what we had to do. Our support system began bogging. I was only in labor for five hours before giving birth to Darnell Jr.; it wasn't so bad. Not one balloon, card, or stuffed animal from Darnell's family. They never visited with Darnell, only Belinda would, but that was because she was Darnell's transportation to the hospital. Of all people, his boss gave us a gift of two hundred dollars. We really appreciated that, considering we'd only known him for a short period of time.

Weeks went by before we rode in the family's car again except to church and taking the boys to and from school, and that was because the twins attended the same school as Carlos' children. I did appreciate the two days Mrs. Matthews's took to help us with some of our priority needs.

Mr. Matthews and I both worked the same hours for the car rental company, so I rode with him. Mrs. Matthews told me her cousin ran a daycare center in her home, and I should give her a call, so I took the opportunity. Everything was working out fine until Mr. Matthews started working overtime. I had to catch a bus that only ran every three hours, and then I had to walk the rest of the way to pick lil Darnell up by 5 p.m. I was always fifteen minutes late and had to pay the late fee at the end of the week. I don't know why in the world I thought the daycare lady would understand my circumstances with her and Mrs. Matthews being cousins. She knew we were fresh in the state and trying hard to accomplish getting fully situated. You'd think she would've been a little more supportive considering we were nearly family, but it was obvious she didn't feel that way, neither did she care.

Darnell would come home from work thinking his family had taken me out house hunting, but they had not. He was disgusted with his family, because they were the main ones encouraging us to relocate to Florida, and he trusted them.

Darnell walked in the rain for hours looking for a house. I received a phone call from a Realtor asking to speak with Darnell, but he hadn't gotten in yet, so I did the talking and negotiating. The Realtor explained that the house needed work, but I didn't care; my goal was to obtain a house and get out of the house where we had been residing for four or five weeks; too long as far as I was concerned. I wasn't used to shacking up at other people's crib, with a family.

The house needed new carpeting, a kitchen sink, and a paint job. It was a single two-bedroom brick house with a huge backyard and a circular driveway in the front yard. Florida was known for its circular driveways, which gave the homes curb appeal. Ours was only large enough for a ten-speed bike, but that was the least of my concerns. Heck, we didn't have a car yet anyway, or a 10 speed bike so I surely wasn't complaining.

God had everything in divine order. Darnell's job had a clearance sale going on, and his boss gave us some of the finest furniture and vases for the flooring. Darnell and his partner delivered furniture to an elderly couple. Rather than a tip, the couple asked the guys to pull up a room full of carpet that she was giving to them as a gift. The couple wanted to revert to ceramic tiling. The carpet was brand-new, like no one had ever walked on it. Darnell's partner didn't need it, so he let us have it all.

We were doing well with the exception of catching the tail end of the hurricanes Florida had to offer. Other than the palmettos, this was another nature issue I didn't like about Florida. Unlike other trees, when heavy winds blew, palm trees only looped over, touching the ground, never breaking or damaging a branch. I was in awe every time I saw that, because it put me in mind of Jesus' triumphant entry into Jerusalem. The crowd spread their garments and palm branches on the road for him in celebration of his coming. The palm tree branches carried the burden of his inevitable journey, and therefore they will always be known for their strength.

We walked three miles to get groceries because of the buses running so many hours apart. Every time we walked that three mile journey to and from the market, I thought about Darnell's family selling us on moving to Florida; how green the grass was on the other side of the fence. I used to have that vision until we actually moved and saw the reality of things. Sometimes it was hard getting a taxi, but one day we lucked up on one. An African man who knew we weren't from around the way got down on us. He charged us ten dollars when it should've been no more than about four bucks. Meters weren't used in Palm Beach county, so he pulled a fast one on us Yankees.

Darnell and I ended up pregnant again with a girl. I jumped for joy and praised God after having four sons. When Darnell's baby mother found out, she had the audacity to tell him "You don't need Amber anymore since you got another daughter." She was a simple, ignorant broad. It wasn't like he was around Amber anyway; they lived in separate states far apart years before Darnell and I met. Once I came into the picture, I bridged all that back together for the support of Amber and I didn't even know her. His baby mama was just a hater and it didn't help that I was seven years younger than her.

11

The Tornado Hits The Roof

I was far along in my pregnancy and had to let my job go, but thank God we were able to buy a vehicle before the loss of income. I was pregnant with my first daughter. I was carrying lil' Darnell on top of my belly in the baby carrier walking miles to and from the market, while at the same time carrying groceries. I truly appreciated a vehicle. The lady who provided daycare in her home gave all the parents one week to find another daycare provider. She used everybody for Christmas cash, but that was okay—everything was in divine order. I wasn't working anymore so I was able to watch my own children. Although Darnell was working, I was still able to receive full benefits from the state. My case worker applauded him for stepping up and telling her he wanted his name on all the paperwork; at first, I looked at that Negro like he was crazy. My case worker said there weren't too many men who would have stepped up to the plate like Darnell did, and she respected him for that, approving us to receive full benefits.

I cleaned up and prepared dinner early. Evening had come

and Darnell hadn't come home from work yet, but I gave him a few more hours because traffic was tail to tail in the state of Florida.

It was 7:30 p.m. and still, no Darnell. The rent was due, and we were already close to being a month late, having to pay a fifty-dollar late fee. We definitely couldn't afford to pay it for the current month's rent. I drove around to places I thought Darnell would be, but still, no luck. I began to worry, because it wasn't like him to hang out, because he didn't know anyone. I drove to the police station to file a missing report. Before the officer gave me the papers, she asked if he had ever come home late before, *"never"* I said. He never hung out late or spent the night out on me, we were still fairly new in the state. The officer asked: "Has he ever used drugs?"

"Years before I met him," I said.

The officer replied, "More than likely that's what he's out doing. Florida is the number one state for drug trafficking and usage."

Driving home, compounded thoughts trampled through my brain like wild animals running for refuge. I tried remaining positive. Darnell relapsing after being drug-free for years was the last thing I wanted to hear. Getting cracked out on me when we were over a thousand miles away from home was way too farfetched for me. We had two small children, an infant, and a baby on the way, and he was the only breadwinner in the house. If the officer was right, which I hoped she wasn't, this was a recipe for disaster. I recapped my thoughts, remembering the first time I'd spoken with Carlos over the phone before relocating. He said, "Florida is the number one drug state in the country. A lot of people who move to Florida get hooked on drugs. Y'all shouldn't come down here!"

Forty-five minutes later Darnell came stumbling in, looking extremely exhausted and out of energy. I asked him where in the heck he had been all this time, but he was so weak he couldn't even answer the question and probably didn't want to. I told him I went to the police station and what the officer said. Darnell reluctantly decided to come clean that he spent all the rent money on crack cocaine.

I was devastated. I was beyond disgusted with him. I needed to know what triggered his mind to go out and do something so stupid as soon as everything fell in place and we were being blessed. It was bad enough not having family support, but we were over that. We were doing great. Darnell reached in his pocket, pulling out a hundred-dollar bill; it was all we had to our name.

I went to the Realtor's to try to handle our situation face-to-face instead of phoning. I figured I stood a better chance if we had eye contact; that's how I was taught to do business. I had to make something up, so I told the Realtor Darnell had been temporarily laid off, but I was sure to have the rent covered within two weeks or less. Unfortunately, he only gave us a week.

Darnell was in too deep; anytime you spend your rent money on drugs, that's a serious problem. I was mentally drained, not knowing what to do next, because everything fell on my shoulders. I didn't even want the thought to cross my mind; *I should've stayed in Detroit.* I wasn't happy there, and now, I was beginning to be unhappy living in Florida too.

The judge gave us seven days to pay two months' rent plus court fees or vacate the premises. I knew we wouldn't have that kind of money in seven days. I used the hundred dollars Darnell gave me to rent a moving truck, pay for storage and one or two nights in motel. The next plan was to find a shelter.

The following Friday when Darnell received his check, he tried to make things right, but it was too late and it wasn't enough. Here I was, with three sons, nine months pregnant, with a daughter, a crack using baby daddy, and no pot to piss in or a window to throw it out of for any of us. I really didn't care if Darnell had anywhere to go, putting his family in such a terrible position, but I had to put my feelings aside. I had no family in the state, and figuratively speaking, neither did he. His family turned their backs on us the first week we were there. We were all we had, and I needed to keep Darnell and his income by my side to help me with the kids and our jacked-up situation.

We continued going to church on Sundays as usual, never mentioning anything about what we were going through; it's not like the Matthews cared. We never learned anything in that church. Every time we stood for the reading and then sat back down to hear the word, all Reverend Matthews did was hold onto that mic and stamp his feet, yelling, "GOD IS GOOD" for a half hour straight. He reminded me of Eddie Murphy in *Coming to America* as Randy Watson yelling out "SEXUAL CHOCOLATE!" Mr. Matthews never elaborated on the scripture he cited. Obviously he knew nothing about the Bible as far as I was concerned, which explained why he had only about ten members—us, his hypocritical household, and maybe three neighbors.

Monday morning the house was cluttered with boxes; it was the day of eviction. I woke up before sunrise and did the two things that don't go hand-n-hand; praying and worrying. I watched my family as they slept on the mattresses we laid out in the family room the night before. I then got them up and we headed out—where? I had no idea. I started making phone calls to shelters, as we drove around in circles without a plan. I kept our quilts and pillows close to us just in case we had to sleep in the car; I had to think twice about spending all we had on a motel. We'd already spent some of what we had to place our belongings in storage.

I found a shelter called The Lord's Place. The administrator said there was a waiting list and even if there wasn't, Darnell wouldn't have been eligible to reside there, because we weren't legally married. I couldn't argue with that. I told the administrator we were just evicted and was hoping he had some leads on other shelters. God immediately touched his heart and he opened up the doors for us. I also believe he took into consideration that Darnell was a working man, and that I was due to go into labor any day. He immediately moved us in and allowed Darnell to reside with us so we could stay together as a family.

We had ninety days to find a home. We were to give two-thirds of our earnings each pay period to be saved toward a new home, and also a third of our food stamps. We were given boxes of dry goods and canned foods every week, and they even offered after-school tutoring programs and activities for the kids. The living standards were unbelievable; everyone had their own private quarters. All quarters offered two bedrooms and two full baths; both rooms had a TV. We had a living and dining room and a kitchen with appliances included, even a dishwasher.

I was still angry with Darnell for putting us through unnecessary stress. I did consider it to be a blessing for my newborn to come home to a place called "The Lord's Place." I didn't tell Darnell my thoughts. I didn't want him getting relaxed, thinking it was okay for his family to dwell in a shelter.

God foretold me in my dream what was going to take place if I moved to Florida, but I was clueless. The tornado snatching the roof from over me and the kids' heads was Darnell, because he being the man of the family is him being head of the house. When I had the dream of Darnell lying in the hospital that was indicating he was sick from having a drug habit. His sickness resulted in us being homeless.

I had a beautiful baby girl with Bette Davis eyes and a head full of dark sandy brown curly hair; I named her Dejah. I gazed at her for a long time, and a thought automatically popped in my head out of nowhere: *You're going to take me through something, I just don't know what!* I had no control over those words. They just came to me.

I was destined to spend time with my one and only daughter. I would make sure she flourished beautifully into her womanhood. I nursed her just like I did the boys. Mother's milk is the best. Not only is it healthy for both the mother and child, but it roots a bond between mother and child that no one can tear apart.

Darnell insisted on smoking crack. He'd lock himself in the bathroom with the vent turned on and window open, just a-pipin' away. I knew nothing other than to pray for him. I didn't know if I was stupid or wise for sticking with him. I was a thousand miles away from home with four children, and knew no one. I loved Darnell and didn't feel right turning my back on him now that he was down and out; we were family and we were all we had. I remembered being destitute before meeting Darnell. He cut the umbilical cord that unstably connected me to Diane, and I began living my womanhood; he flew me from the cuckoos nest. That meant a lot to me!

Darnell and I were referred to a lady named Jessica who rented us a two-bedroom home. She seemed fairly professional, but not too friendly, which I understood considering her managerial position. Jessica sent us to meet at her mother's house because she was the owner of the property. Mrs. Morgan looked more evil than the devil himself. Mr. Morgan was a brick layer, quiet and subtle. I could tell Mr. Morgan was henpecked; I would assume so from the aura that scented them both. There was something about Mrs. Morgan that was evil and wicked. She got straight to the point, took care of business very quickly, gave us our keys, and introduced us back to the front door; no smile, good-byes, or no nothing.

The neighbors were decent and they had children as well. The area was nice and clean other than an old garbage can lid that lay on the ground outside the complex. My side of the street was the only line of houses, and across the street were woods.

The twins started their new school and I signed them up for the after-school program. I was still a stay-at-home mom while Darnell continued working every day to provide for us. Everyday I would sit in the yard holding my daughter. I'd watched lil' Darnell struggle to shoot the ball in his basketball hoop, and whenever he was tired he'd sit on top of ball to rest; he didn't want to share it.. Every now and again I glanced up to the sky. I could feel down in my spirit our journey in Florida was dying down; I could smell a new season coming on. Darnell's drug habit wasn't getting any better, and talking with Daevon on a regular basis and hearing the sadness in his voice was dawning on me. He was having bad dreams every night; the longer I was gone the more he cried for me. Diane had plans to send him down to live with us. She knew nothing we were going through, and I needed for it to stay that way.

The only time I pursued peace was spending nights at the beach. The family and I stretched out in lawn chairs with blankets and pillows, watching the bright moon shimmer across the Atlantic Ocean all night. I'd lay there reminiscing when Mr. Matthews baptized me and the twins in that salty ocean; it was our first time ever being baptized.

Not only were things dying down for me in Florida, but I had come to reality that we had moved right in the heart of drug city. Although Darnell didn't know anyone to cop from, our next-door neighbor Meechie did. I was too embarrassed. I started spending money more freely. I think it was my way of dealing with my burdens like Darnell reverting to crack to deal with whatever it was he was going through. It still wasn't justifiable. I just couldn't come to grips with him back-sliding after we relocated over a thousand miles away from home, and after years of sobriety. I didn't look down on him; I just wished he had used his brain for a better resource other than frying it. I thought he possibly could've relapsed, because he felt like his family turned their backs on him and he felt as if he had to carry the world on his shoulders. Not only did they let him down, but us too, his immediate family. He probably thought about what Diane and my dad would think if they knew. It's no telling what went through his mind, because how we were treated was totally unexpected. We didn't ask to move to Florida, we were asked to move to Florida.

For me, hanging out was the easy way out, so I started going places with Meechie and her family. I needed time away from the housewife life, so I went to bingo every other night and to the Florida State Fair. I hung out so much, steadily spending money that I didn't realize how quick the Christmas season had come.

Meechie and I went shopping for the kids. When we got home and sat down I began looking stupid, because I spent all the rent money on gifts. I decided I had to engage in unethical activities; hustling the toy store. I grabbed my receipt and returned to the store's back entrance. I grabbed a buggy and put every toy listed on my receipt back in the buggy. I walked straight to the service desk and handed the cashier the receipt to return the toys in the basket I hadn't even paid for. I was returned every penny with no problem. Meechie was scared, but I wasn't. I was hungry. I was surviving.

Come the night before Christmas, I sat by the tree glancing at all the gifts. I reorganized them and noticed every gift had holes punctured in it and was flipped on the opposite side. Kids do the darndest things!

Darnell approached his boss about a loan, which wasn't the first time. Darnell was fired on the spot, because his boss felt that Darnell wasn't providing for his family like he should have. Darnell borrowing money and losing weight gave his boss insight....at least that's what I believe. He had been watching Darnell for some time, noticing a difference in his demeanor. When he came home and told me what his boss said, it devastated me; the last thing we needed was a loss of income.

Darnell immediately applied for unemployment. Thank God he was eligible.

We were short on the rent which had been about our fourth time. For some odd reason I didn't think it would be a problem with the landlord, because that was extra money for them with the charge of late fees and all. Once we did come up with the rest, we tried reaching Jessica, but she never responded, so we stopped by Mrs. Morgan's place, and she was intoxicated as usual. We stepped in and Darnell reached out to hand her the rent money. Mrs. Morgan had totally flipped the script. *"Don't walk up on me!"* Darnell looked at me and we both were skeptical of what to do from there. She didn't accept the rent and told us to take it up with Jessica.

We called Jessica and left one message after another; days had gone by and we still hadn't heard from her. I couldn't understand why the sudden change with the family. Other than being late with the rent, the only other thing I could come up with was someone probably snitched to the Morgans about Darnell's habit. They knew everyone, because they owned the majority of the complexes in the small town. We called Mrs.

Morgan again, hoping to rectify the situation, but she bluntly said that her daughter wasn't going to accept the rent. I asked if it was because we were late, but she hung up. We prepared ourselves to move once again.

Meechie said the Morgans did her mother the same way, and that's why they were living with their aunt. She said that they were always strange people who had very little compassion and communication with anybody unless it had to do with business only. When we finally spoke with Jessica, she gave us the famous seven-day eviction notice. I definitely wasn't going to court, knowing they had connections with the sheriff, attorneys, and judges; we wouldn't have stood a chance at winning. I just made a phone call to Diane, letting her know that we would be moving back soon. I knew it would bring happiness to her versus losing Daevon to a thousand miles from home. She was in the process of moving out of her house because it was too much for her to handle financially, as usual. I hated falling right back in Diane's trap, but I didn't have much time to plan. I had to bite the dust. We were busted in Florida. I thought about DMX when he chanted to Nas on *Belly*, "Here we go again."

> *Many of us crucify ourselves between*
> *two thieves: regret for the past and*
> *fear of the future.*
> *Fulton Oursler*

12

An Act of God

Meechie and I were sitting in the front yard talking and laughing. The kids were running and playing, and even my daughter Dejah ran around in her walker. I just so happened to look towards the right and noticed the garbage can lid still lying in the same place it was when I first moved into the complex so I got up to move it. As soon as I lifted the lid, over fifty palmettos scattered everywhere "OH MY GOD!" I snatched my daughter up from her walker and started jumping and ducking all over the place. It was an open sewage filled with urine and feces. The sewage hole was wide enough for an adult to fall right in, let alone a toddler.

"Meechie, did you know there was a sewage drain in the front yard, and if so how come you haven't mentioned anything to the landlord about it?" I couldn't get a straight answer, which led me to believe the family was afraid of being evicted again. The Morgan family was people of power, and Meechie probably felt the need to protect the roof over their heads. There was no telling how long that lid had been there. Other than Meechie and her family, previous renters were probably afraid to open their mouths too, but not me. I didn't care how much power the Morgan family had and not only that; we were already evicted so I really didn't care. People's lives were in danger just standing in the front yard. The Morgans were nasty and cruel. They were a very evil hearted family. You could definitely see the demon in Mrs. Morgan.

I notified the Health Department and they were there in twenty minutes. The next morning Mr. Morgan had the sewage sealed for safety. He was a brick layer, so there was no reason that sewage should have been unsealed right in the front yard in the first place; how trifling. I would've called Mrs. Morgan myself, but she wasn't answering my phone calls—probably too busy getting drunk and being the evil witch she naturally was.

My family and I moved the day after the repair. I truly believed that it was an act of God as to why we moved there in the first place; everything happens for a reason. No one else spoke out, knowing the sewage lay there not properly secured. I understand they were probably afraid of being evicted. There were millions of places to rent in the state of Florida. A child's life, you simply cannot replace!

We were indecisive about who we trusted to retrieve our mail. Everything was moving so fast, and our only option was Belinda or Diane. Diane was always trying to destroy me, and Belinda spent the money we wired to her for our security deposit, but did pay it back. We didn't want to trust either of them, but had to trust somebody, so we sent our mail to Belinda's house until we were settled back in Detroit.

Darnell wrote a sizzling hot check to place our belongings in storage and another one to spend one night at a hotel. The next day we drove to his job to retrieve his last paycheck and checked into a motel for a month until he received his taxes and back to the "D" we went.

13

A Pastor is Only Human; He's Not God

It felt so good embracing my firstborn son again. Watching Daevon as he was reunited with his brothers was a breathtaking moment. Siblings should never have to experience being separated from one another, and especially being from the same mother, and at such a young age. Long story short; Diane willingly gave me back full custody of Daevon. She realized that a large part of his heart was completely hallow where as, me and his siblings filled that void.

Diane knew Darnell and I weren't working with much income, so she was willing to work with us. I couldn't believe how humble Diane had become. She had plans to lay down new carpet and have other repairs done once we started paying rent.

Two months back in the "D" we knew everything should've been transferred and in the system for Darnell's unemployment benefits to start kicking in. We were expecting to receive a lump sum back, until we found out that Belinda had stolen every check and cashed them at the bank's drive-thru. The banks in Florida didn't have surveillance cameras, and identification wasn't required. We were unfortunate in pressing charges, because the theft took place in Florida, and according to the authorities that's where the charges had to be filed. We definitely didn't have money to hire a lawyer. I was so full of grief; not only could we not catch up in rent, but we lost our entire storage. I let go and let God! Imma' keep it real; He wasn't pleased with me stealing all those Christmas gifts. I believe He blew on all our money. I had to pay for my sins and my family had to suffer the consequences for my thoughtless actions. However, Belinda was going to pay for her sins as well.

Looking at what used to be my old neighborhood, I saw that it hadn't changed much besides a few new neighbors here and there. Tidus was still running the corner store and that was a good thing. I knew I could get Darnell a job working there like I did for Gino. I started working afternoons in downtown Detroit as a telemarketer in the call center. I took the bus to work and Diane picked me up so I wouldn't have to catch the bus in late-night hours.

A month later Diane started getting tired of picking me up, so I ended up having to take the bus anyway. She had a bad habit of turning her back on me right before I could get on my feet, but as usual I wasn't surprised; that was Diane's signature. She could've given us time to buy a vehicle, but no, she just made sure we were caught up with most of our rent and the heck with everything else. Darnell had to put the kids to sleep, and then walk to the bus stop so I wouldn't have to walk the mile home alone in the middle of the night. However, after a month I felt the need to quit that job, because Darnell and I didn't feel comfortable leaving the kids home every night.

I quickly found a daytime job working for the phone company and Tidus switched Darnell from days to evenings. When

I came in from work, Darnell was headed out for work.

We found another family church home and by the grace of God they provided us with transportation back and forth to Sunday and midweek services. We loved our new church home, because we were finally getting the word of God. Peace was starting to hover over us; we were headed on a path to righteousness, and I was hoping it would start with Darnell's drug habit.

Eventually he stopped using completely, but he was still drinking like a fish. I know it was challenging for him, and I was there every step of the way. I believed Darnell was facing spiritual warfare. A spiritual warfare is an individual journey; a battle within yourself that only God can help you with, and that's if you want the help. I kept praying for Darnell and continued encouraging him; that was all I knew to do.

I tried ignoring the repetitious dreams of Dejah getting hit by a car; it was starting to get too overwhelming. In the dream I was praying and panicking at the same time while running to her rescue, pulling her from underneath the vehicle, and every time she would still be alive. I always woke up breathless and panicking. Darnell always held me tight, comforting me, and assuring me that everything would be all right. All I could do was trust that Jesus would make everything all right. I still didn't fully understand how faith worked. I just knew God was real, and Jesus was his son. I held on to what I knew. No matter how much I prayed, the fear of Dejah getting hit by a car wouldn't go away; it only got more and more intense. I still trusted God though!

God blessed our family financially and we were finally able to catch up on what little we owed on the rent. The new month was in a few days, so we didn't pay that month's rent, because we knew Diane was happy enough with two G's in the palm of her hand. Once the two G's left from my hand to hers, all that talk about renovating the house went right out the window. She took that money and went on a vacation with my aunt Lynne to Venezuela. When she returned home she was broke, and the first stop was to me and Darnell to ask for more money. I looked at Diane like she had lost her mind. True enough the rent was due, but dang, she was sucking us dry. I could understand if we weren't taking care of business, but we were. It's like Diane didn't want us to have anything, just only enough to get by. She always wanted to be in control constantly trying to keep up with me and Darnell's business. Diane treated me like Pinocchio, and as if I was incompetent. If I was incompetent it was because of her not teaching me the woes of life. She raised me to get an education, yes she did, but the facts of life I did not know, and that's how she wanted me so I could fail and run to her for refuge; back under her control. Diane knew how to survive, she knew the struggle and the streets; she was definitely about that life.

I remember one Thanksgiving holiday she dropped Daevon off with me, and my aunt dropped her son off as well. I also had other children of the family including my own. I had no stove at the time to cook on, and was wondering what I was going to do. My best friend Ladondra had an old range she wasn't using, and she sacrificed bringing it over the night before Thanksgiving so my family could have a feast for the holiday. It was the kind that had a second oven attached above the range. The lower oven didn't work only the attached one above, but there were no baking racks to place the baking dishes on and none of the eyes lit up. Darnell stayed up all night scrubbing and trying to get the lower oven and all eyes working. He did all he could to make miracles happen with the range, but could only get one eye to work so we appreciated that and worked with what we had.

I was up at 4 a.m. preparing a meal for my family while Darnell was out doing his thing! I took a wire hanger and folded it into a rack, somehow tying it up in the oven so I could potentially cook more than one dish at a time. Diane called me a little after 3 p.m., asking how things were going, in hopes of hearing that I was struggling with my dinner. She boastfully said, "We're done cooking," and I peacefully said, "We're done eating." She was literally pissed! She couldn't believe how that was even possible; "How are you done eating already?"

Pastor Raymond took Darnell and me to search for a vehicle; we were desperate for transportation. We bought a conversion van and guess what happened two weeks later? Our gas line somehow got contaminated; how weird was that? I didn't think once to blame Diane, knowing she was good for being evil. I still believe she had something to do with me and Darnell's first vehicle that got smacked out in front of her house when we lived with her. So once again, we were without transportation.

Church was serving dinner after service. Pastor Raymond made it plain and clear that those who lived in sin were not welcome to fellowship after service. We were to take our food home and eat; only the single people (who he thought were saving their body as a temple) and the married couples were welcome to fellowship. Over half the church, including the pastor's very own son, took home carry-outs. Pastor Raymond was out of order for that. Everyone should have taken a plate home, including him. One sin commits them all; you can't exclude just one sin. Everybody in the world sins Pastor Raymond! Every now and then Darnell stayed at home with kids while I attended midweek service, so the pastor would drive me home, alone. He always asked about my personal life concerning Darnell and me, and it wasn't out of concern, but for his own personal motive. Pastor Raymond complimented my curves and I dressed modestly; I could tell he was on some other stuff. I watched his eyes out the corner of mines, as they wandered in all the wrong places on my body. I watched how he undressed me with his eyes; I knew what he wanted! I wasn't comfortable, and it wasn't just the fact of him being a married man, but it was weird being indirectly flirted with by my very own pastor. I looked up to him spiritually. However, it was easy to ignore him, because he only drove me home maybe twice a month. I also loved my church home and didn't want to stop serving the Lord there, because I needed God to work on my relationship.

Saturday night I couldn't sleep. I kept waking up every two hours drenched in sweat, and my heart pounding from panic attacks. My blood tingled throughout my entire body from nervousness, and my spirit was weary and restless. Sunday morning we didn't attend church because I was so tired. I needed to sleep.

Arielle and my Godchildren spent the weekend, so later that afternoon she decided to take the kids for a walk. She had a baseball league full of kids, and there was only one other adult to help chaperone. I suggested my children stay home, but she insisted on taking them to the park to stretch and run around while I got some rest.

"SHINICE, SHINICE!" was all I heard coming up the block. The lady who helped chaperone the kids came banging on my door like the FBI. "OH MY GOD, KEEVON JUST GOT HIT BY A CAR." Immediately I felt tranquilized; Jesus came to my comfort, and immediately I began to feel calm and was confident that my son was okay. I tried calming Arielle's friend down so I could ask her the one important question: "Is he dead?"

"No," she replied, and that was all I needed to hear; I could

definitely work with that. I ran to the corner to see Keevon lying on the corner with his leg broken in two places. I kneeled
down to comfort him and assure him that everything would
be okay. He was in shock for the moment with all the people
hovering over him screaming, and some were crying. Before I
came outside Keevon was lying in the street, because no one
wanted to move him, potentially causing worse damage to his
leg. Arielle, however, moved him out of fear of him possibly
getting hit again, and I thank her...she did the right thing.
The lady who hit him immediately stopped at the scene. The
paramedics arrived and took Keevon to the hospital and the
lady stayed close behind, following us to emergency.

Diane forced me into suing. I had no intentions of suing
that lady; she was driving under the speed limit, and it was an
unfortunate mistake. That lady was just as nervous as Keevon
was, and was genuinely concerned about my child's life. Diane
felt that even though it was a mistake, we needed to take action
anyway, because Keevon's condition could recur and potentially worsen in the future. Diane said if I didn't sue, she would,
and I couldn't give her power to do that because my son definitely wasn't going to benefit from it. I sued for that purpose
only, and told the lady as I sincerely apologized for it. That was
the least of her cares; she was fully insured and her sole concern
was my son's health and future.

Arielle told the kids to get ready to cross, not cross the street!
Keevon dodged right across the street before Arielle could say
anything else, that's why my children should've stayed home;
there were too many kids and not enough adults. Thank God
the lady was driving under the speed limit. You could literally
jog alongside of her car, that's how slow she was going according to witnesses.

I called Pastor Raymond and told him what had happened.

He asked me what time the accident took place, and I said: "just after 2:00 p.m." Pastor Raymond said: "The incident happened during service, and if you all had been in church it would not have happened." I kept my respect for my so-called-shepherd, listened, and politely ended the conversation. I never attended that church again. I was flabbergasted! There was no love lost and I forgave him!

Early Tuesday morning the phone rang. It was Carmen's voice on the other end, and she didn't ask how I was doing or anything. She came right out and asked me to come to Tennessee for the weekend, which was four days away. She had moved there during the time Darnell and I had moved to Florida. She always had a way of getting what she wanted from me, because she knew how much I loved her; she was my only sister. I prepared myself for the trip.

> *Not many of you should become teachers,*
> *my fellow believers, because you*
> *know that we who teach*
> *will be judged more strictly.*
> *James 3:1*

14

Hustling: Back to The Dirty-Dirty

It was pure hell on the highway to Tennessee. Traffic was bumper to bumper due to the tornado weather. It was raining extremely hard, and the wind was traveling at least forty to fifty miles per hour. All the kids were sleep, and I was driving because Darnell had ten drinks too many. It was pitch-black on the highway other than the headlights and brake lights from the other vehicles. I couldn't figure out how to turn my headlights on because we had rented a caravan, and I guess, maybe, we should've checked all that amenity stuff before driving, but we didn't. I was driving with parking lights on only and couldn't see anything. I was extremely irritated to the point I wanted to kick Darnell out on the highway and keep driving. It was hell driving in the midst of tornado weather, and he was drunk asleep; I hated him for that!

Carmen lived in a private division in Tennessee, which contained a two-block secluded area with approximately forty homes. All of the homes were structured in colonial or ranch style with four bedrooms, two full baths, central air, and all appliances included. I was excited about seeing Carmen and the kids, as it had been a few years.

I was impressed with Tennessee. Inhaling the south's aroma was peaceful, as if our ancestors were giving us a warm welcome back home. I noticed when driving on the highway, the minute we hit the south's borderline, the heaviness that weighed my shoulders lifted and fled into the wind. I never felt so light-weight in all my days; I felt like a feather, like my burdens were left back with the city life.

I loved the dark back roads and the glowing eyes from the deer that peeked through from the woods. If you weren't used to driving these roads, it was easy to run off into a ditch, being unfamiliar with the twists and turns. Carmen knew the back roads like the back of her hand, but it didn't stop her from running over a deer that stood in the middle of the road like it owned it. She was rushing to hang out on a Friday night when BAAM! She smacked the deer and it lay on the side of the road half dead. All she had was a fender bender and 140 heartbeats a second. That's jail time in the south when you hit any animal and run. They have just as much equal opportunity as people; it's called animal rights. Carmen wasn't trying to risk her freedom for a darn deer. She was too busy trying to make it to the club before 10:00 p.m. The club special for the night was *get in free and sip on two-dollar drinks all night*. Carmen had clubs to hang at Sunday through Saturday. Every time she stepped out I thought about MC Breed's "Let's Go to the Club."

Carmen's whole plan was to ask me to relocate so she wanted me to drive down and physically experience the environment. She told me and Darnell about the plant that was hiring, and it wasn't far, only down the road a piece as the southerners would describe it. She said it was the season for hire, and the pay and benefits were excellent. She also said the state needed people to sign up for Section 8, that they were practically begging people to apply.

The next morning the sound of an ostrich awoke me; it lived one yard over. I thought they belonged on a farm. I just lay there soaking in the idea of relocating again while tossing and turning.

Carmen suggested Darnell and I fill out applications for the job and apply for Section 8. There were at least eight vacancies in her vicinity ready for rent. We spent our weekend potentially preparing to relocate. I weighed my options, what would be the best choice for my family's stability and financial situation?

It wasn't as rough breaking the news to Diane as it was the first time. I think she was ready for us to move anyway, and I definitely wasn't going to wait and be thrown out into the streets. I was going to be in control of making the move this time. The neighbor across the street was sitting on her front porch; she and her children lived with her parents. I walked over and told her that I was moving out, and would talk to Diane about renting the house to her. Her brother Deon lived next door to me. I remember him telling me when his family moves they usually all move together on the same street. Looking into her eyes gave me the impression that she was the black sheep of the family. She looked miserable and stressed out, like she'd been through a lot. I hadn't actually visualized any trouble with any of the family, so that's why I felt compassion in my heart to speak to Diane on her behalf. I was cool with her family, and Diane communicated with them as well. She appreciated how they maintained their homes inside and out and that there was never any drama; that was a good sign to Diane.

It was about time to gas up so we could move on to the

next chapter in life, so we hit the next exit and pulled up to the pumps. I entered my debit card and was declined because my card was maxed. WHAT? I had only sixty-three dollars in cash to my name. I used the pay phone to call my bank. I waited nearly ten minutes before speaking to a representative, and God knows I didn't have extra money to be sticking in that phone booth. The representative finally came on the line to access my account, only to tell me that my card was maxed out. I was completely flabbergasted! I'd just checked my balance the morning before we left. I panicked, because we were near the borderline of Ohio and Kentucky with only sixty-three dollars. We had two vehicles, one of which was a gas-guzzling moving truck; the largest one, might I add! Darnell tried calming me down, but I wasn't trying to hear that. I took all the money I had and split the gas between both vehicles. I was hoping possibly by the time we needed filling up again the card would transact. Although Darnell didn't have one jittery finger or a blink of an eye, I immediately started to blame him.

As we drove back on the highway, all kinds of thoughts began trampling through my head. My brain felt like it was cracking from a massive earthquake, knowing that there was no turning back. I literally had no choice but to allow my faith to kick in, because I knew this was the move that God had in store for us. I knew God had a house for us, that good-paying job and Section 8 waiting for us. I wasn't going to let the devil discourage me. I wasn't going to allow him to steal what God had in store for me and my family. I kept saying to myself, *What God has for me is for me!*

It was impossible that Darnell could have spent that money because I had the card. Even if he did relapse and get a hold of our card, there was no way he could've spent over two G's in one night. I found myself recapturing the past, thinking about all he had taken me and the kids through when he was on drugs. Darnell had me on defense at all times. If I misplaced a dime or a dollar, he was to blame, but the majority of the time I found myself apologizing for it later when I ended up finding it. I couldn't help the lack of trust I had in him.

We exited to a nearby gas station just past the Kentucky state line; this time only the truck needed refilling. Again I tried using the card reader, and sure enough it read maximum exceeded. I told Darnell to get out of the truck and drive the car to another parking area. I had to put on the role of a single woman with children, because I stood a stronger chance of getting help. As embarrassing as it sounds, and as it was to me, I had to set my pride aside and get my hustle on.

I walked over to a truck driver who was gassing up and introduced myself. I started explaining my situation timidly and using my voice seductively as I asked for money. I didn't want the truck driver thinking I was just some random lot lizard hustling him in any way. I was so embarrassed; I didn't know what was going through that man's mind, but I didn't have time to worry about it either. I had to do what I had to do! I've never had a drop of prejudice blood in my body, but I did not feel comfortable asking a white man for money in the state of Kentucky. I heard how prejudice white people can be in the south versus up north; that a lot of them hate black people. Little did I know he had so much compassion. He was genuinely concerned and very understanding, knowing I had children with me.

He walked over to the pump, inserted his credit card into the card reader, and gassed the truck to the "F" mark. I didn't want him to feel any discomfort in thinking I might try to rob him or read his account number. I kept my back facing him, thanking Jesus, and continuing my polite conversation with him. I thanked the man repeatedly! It was nothing but a thing to him, and that's what God loves, a cheerful giver. I was truly grateful. I offered my cell number, and I had every intention of paying him back with interest, but like I said, it was nothing to him. Never, ever judge a person by their skin color!

Darnell felt bad, and I didn't care until I had gotten to the bottom of what happened to over two thousand dollars. We were moving again, and not just to another neighborhood, but another state. I never forgot what my caseworker told me back in Florida. "You may have to let him go, let him hit rock bottom to make him appreciate his family."

We were less than two hours away from Tennessee; the rental was at a half tank of gas and the truck needed a full refill again. We exited to another and hopefully the last gas station, but no luck because when we pulled up to the front, it was all boarded up.

I continued watching signs for the next service station sign, and the next one was in another thirty miles. I was so pissed at Darnell I didn't know what to do. Paranoid and worried like crazy, wondering if the truck would run out of gas on the thirty-mile journey. God brought us thus far, so I couldn't give up. I had to keep the faith and keep pressing on, because there was definitely no turning back; literally...there was no turning back! It was like entering a haunted house—you're petrified and adamant about going back toward a door with no knob. You just gotta keep the faith and keep it moving forward!

Thank God we made it. The little gas we had was just enough to go thirty miles. I repeated the same story to the next truck driver, but to my surprise Darnell stepped up to the plate and introduced himself. We both told the trucker the truth, because either he was going to help or not. I knew God was going to make a way out of no way; look how far we had traveled, and he saw us through over half the way. Although I was worried, I knew He wasn't going to see us stranded in the middle of nowhere. The truck driver and his partner graciously gave us thirty dollars, and again I was so embarrassed. I was also very grateful, and I strived to keep my head up as Darnell and I thanked them both repeatedly. I rushed into the gas station to pay for my fill-up, and then rushed back out to the pump, hoping the truckers were still outside. I needed them to see how truthful we were by gassing up the entire thirty dollars right in front of them.

We prayed the half tank of gas in the rental would be enough to get us to our one-way destination. I prayed all the way!

> *I don't believe in magic, I believe in miracles*
> *I don't believe in good luck, I believe in God's*
> *Grace.*
> *Sherese L. Jordan*

15

Faith's Results

We finally arrived with both vehicles very low on fuel. Carmen, Malcolm, and the kids came outside and greeted us with warm, happy welcomes, unlike Darnell's family in Florida. I was really happy to see Carmen and the kids that I had actually forgotten all that we had been through.

We all drove to the nearest service station to gas up both rentals. The kids grabbed all kinds of junk food, tossing it on the counter for the attendant to scan. I reached for my ATM card, totally forgetting the highway-hustling. She ran it through and handed me a receipt to sign, and that's when it all came back to me. I was beyond relieved. I called the bank to get clarity as to why I couldn't accomplish any transactions. The problem was too many transactions within a 24-hour period, so there was a block placed on my card for security purposes. I was the one who made all the transactions, purchasing everything we needed for the move. I apologized to Darnell at once. I felt like if he had never taken me through what he did in the past, I wouldn't have been so protective with the money in the first place.

The apartment manager was running a half-month move-in special, so if we waited until the fifteenth of the month we could move in free and the security deposit would be waived. The fifteenth was only two days away so that's what we did, because it saved us over a thousand dollars in moving costs.

On the highway driving back to Carmen's house, there was a student driver taking a road test, and wasn't driving fast enough for Sheila and Carmen. They decided to speed past him and I followed, because I didn't know where I was going. Two miles ahead stood a State Patrol officer in the middle of the highway, blowing his whistle and ordering us all to pull over. The officer could barely write up traffic tickets because he had a serious nervous condition. While we waited for our tickets, the same student driver passed us by; we ended up driving behind him after all.

Carmen and Malcom led Darnell to the truck rental company. Darnell's intentions were to drop the truck off after hours, because we didn't tell the rental company we were driving it out of state. We didn't want to spend eight hundred unnecessary dollars to rent the truck one way so we did it our way. We kept the car rental longer than we should have in order to take care of as much business as we could to get settled down. Carmen and Malcom were pissed at Darnell—they didn't know he was going to just drop the truck off like that. They thought they were in the middle of drama. I can tell you this: She didn't have a problem driving our rental car around whenever she wanted, and knew the police were looking for it because we were two weeks late turning it in.

By the time the police located my whereabouts and inquired about the rental, we had already turned it in. I gave him a location and told him I turned it in late. They couldn't do anything if we weren't physically in the car, so I wasn't worried.

Sheila allowed us to keep her vehicle for a week to take care of the rest of our business. I knew she trusted me, and she sensed that Darnell was a good man, and welcomed him as family. She did tell me that Darnell was overprotective over me, and would go to the ends of the world for me. She saw that in him, and didn't even know him; I didn't even see that, all the years we had been together. I didn't know if that was good or bad. Love can be strange: it can cause people to do strange things.

I applied for food stamps, at least until our jobs came through; we needed all that was offered, because two thousand dollars was only going to take us so far. When we were approved, we received over eight hundred dollars in retro. I filled my kitchen and deep freezer. I shared with Carmen and her mother, Sheila. Sheila was humble, but not Carmen; she had to go spend over two hundred dollars. It was okay, she was my only sister, and she knew how to get her way with me; I actually thought it was cute!

I was offered a position at the plant we applied for, and then a week later Darnell was offered one. I took the morning shift while he took afternoons. The only hang-up about the job was the lay-offs; if you didn't have seniority, you were liable to get a pink slip without notice. I gave Darnell his props for bringing home his entire paycheck and giving it to me. I was hoping and praying he didn't relapse again; I was vigilant and holding on to thoughts of "what ifs" in the back of my mind.

I was turned down from Section 8 housing authorities, because of my income. The intake worker rescheduled me a week later, but I was turned down again. The third time I was asked to take a few days off, and then bring in that pay stub and she would be able to help me. Tennessee State was nearly begging people to apply for subsidized housing; while in the meantime, Michigan's Section 8 program had been closed for over five years.

I had faith God would see us through on the long drive down, and as a result we were showered with blessings. I had begun to understand why my family and I had such a hard struggle getting to Tennessee. God had great blessings in store for us that the devil didn't want us to have. We all know the common saying; what God has for me, is for me!

16

Sheeps in Wolves Clothing

Darnell and I were in need of a vehicle. I asked Carmen how strict were the company's policy in terms of late rent payments. Carmen said, "Oh girl, they ain't gone say nothing. It's not like you gone be a month late. I'm waitin' to pay mines next week too."

Sheila and I drove around in search of a vehicle. The only downfall about living in the south was the lack of public transportation, other than taxicab services. Buses didn't run outside the cities in Tennessee. I didn't want to continue being dependent upon anyone else's transportation. Sheila took me to the same car lot where she purchased her car. She picked the car out, and that was the end of it; just like my daddy, persistent and persuasive. She knew my taste in cars just like my daddy.

When we pulled onto the block, I finally saw the neighborhood kids outside. They probably were looking out the window everyday watching my kids play around. I hadn't seen any children out playing since we moved there. We always brought life to any block we lived on. Before you knew it, all the kids were out playing together every day. I was the witty one and the best young chef on the block. The neighbors loved my cooking and my dark humor. All of us mothers started spending time with one another. If one pulled out a barbeque grill, we all pulled one out except Carmen; she was too busy waiting on me to cook and stealing my recipes, lol!

Once in a while Darnell, the kids and I would attend Sheila's church, although we didn't attend like we should have. The kids enjoyed the first church they started attending when we first moved to Tennessee, because the children were more of a substantial focus. Every Sunday they came home eager to tell us what they learned, and show off all the prizes they won, along with picture drawings, arts and crafts.

The news had been broadcasting a tornado watch, which was a natural disaster I wasn't used to back in the city. Southern states are most known for their Mother Nature catastrophes. Detroit was always known as the murder capital or the "Hell City." If you didn't know God, you were gonna get to know him or allow life to defeat you, and meet him face-to-face immediately. By all means, don't get it twisted, I love the "D"; I was born and raised there. But it was a stressful city to live in, because so many people live scandalously, with so much hate and anger. Some people walked around like zombies, demented from life itself. You're liable to get shot at just for looking at someone. The "D" gives you two options to get to know God. Pray all day and everyday out of fear to keep you safe from getting hurt or killed, or get to know God willingly so he can control your temper and keep you from hurting or killing somebody!

I begged Darnell to stay home from work because of the tornado watch, but unfortunately he didn't. He was confident that we would be okay; he was from the South, so he was used to it. I wasn't used to that type of weather. When we lived in Florida, all we got was the tail end, and it was nothing compared to what was expected to arrive in Tennessee. I had been talking back and forth with Carmen and Malcolm over the phone to keep updated on the weather, which was increasing vigorously. Malcolm suggested I take a twin mattress inside the walk-in closet to cover our heads.

A few minutes later Carmen and her kids pulled into my driveway, blowing the horn like crazy. She was yelling for us to go to Sheila's place, which I hadn't yet had the pleasure of seeing. Carmen said her place was much safer than ours.

We pulled in front of a one-story brick apartment. Sheila came running to the front door, screaming, "HURRY, HURRY, IT'S ALMOST HERE!" Carmen and the kids and I ran into the apartment as the courageous sounds of the wind blew wickedly. "WHERE WILL WE TAKE COVER?" I yelled.

"The bathtub!" Sheila said. I knew darn well they didn't expect all eleven of us to get in one bathtub! Sheila's eyes grew extremely large as she looked across the sky. "WE NEED TO TAKE COVER, NOWWW!"

I gazed up into the sky over to my left and saw a mixture of black, hot pink, purple, and gray colors coat the skies. I grabbed my kids, got back in the car, and took off like a bat out of hell, scared to death and mad as heck. I was petrified as thoughts trampled through my brain. The bathtub? How in the world did she expect eleven Negros to fit in one freakin' bathtub with nothing to grab hold of but a spout and two knobs? I didn't mean to think so harshly, but I was pissed. I thought about when Carmen first called and asked me to come and visit her, like she lived in the next neighborhood over or something. I had to drive in tornado weather then. Every time I took advice from Carmen or Arielle about a major situation something crazy always happened. Here I was again, in a jacked up situation, driving with my kids, and potentially a tornado on my tail. I had to cross over the bridge to get back home. I couldn't see the construction lines and rarely could see the stone walls on either side of the shoulders. I was the only dummy on the streets.

When we arrived back home, the news broadcasted that the tornado was headed our way, less than twenty miles away. I grabbed the family Bible my dad gave us and placed it in the center of the living room floor. The kids formed a circle, held hands, and prayed while I ran upstairs to grab a twin mattress from one of the bunk beds. Once I had the mattress in place, I joined my children and we prayed long and powerfully. I had some praying kids. I taught them Psalms 23, and The Lord's Prayer at the age of three. The harder we prayed, the crazier the wind blew, and the rain blew furiously across the air. The last thing we heard the anchorman say was the tornado had jumped from one city straight over to ours, and there, that's when our power went out. That was one of the scariest moments in my life. I was crying and almost panicked, but I kept praying strong. The kids were praying even harder with eyes shut tight. They were focusing on the faith they had in our prayers, versus the fear of the tornado. Their faith was larger than a mustard seed; literally, they were my strength at that very moment.

Out of nowhere the dark multicolored skies turned clear blue in the blink of an eye. I cried praises to God, while embracing my children and thanking them for being my praying warriors, especially Raheem. We never made it to the closet. Darnell served in the U.S. Army, so he distilled that firm discipline in the boys; it was deeply rooted in him. He raised the boys to be soldiers, to never cry and always protect their mother, and that's what they did. When he came in from work the first thing he said was "I told you y'all would be all right!"

I received a letter from the Realtor's lawyer; they were suing me for one month's rent. I spoke with the lawyer's secretary and she explained that there was a strict policy with the renting agency. I owed over two thousand dollars in rent, lawyer, court fees, and interest. I had to have all paid in full before my court date, was less than four weeks. I was so disgusted! I believed Darnell and I were taken advantage of, just because they knew we had good-paying jobs. There was no way we should have had to come out of over two grand.

I called Carmen and she had the same letter, owing almost eight hundred dollars. I regretted listening to her, but it was too late for all that. Again, I took advice from Carmen and ended up sinking in quicksand. I asked if she needed me to help her financially because I didn't want her to lose her house. She was only working part time, and Malcolm wasn't working at all, but she said she would be fine. I moved south partly on account of her and didn't want to take a chance on us potentially being separated in two different cities.

The month was almost up and Darnell and I paid everything off. Again I thought, *This was a conspiracy!* I believe it was a way to plunge Darnell and me out of money as the Realtor figured we could afford the expenses. Everybody knew everybody and they all worked together. The housing agencies, lawyers, doctors, officers, bail bondsmen, and judges were all connected; they were one big powerful financial franchise.

When I arrived back from the real estate company, I pulled into my driveway. Carmen came walking up to me in need of over seven hundred dollars at the last minute. I looked at her like she was crazy. "Carmen, I told you if you needed help to let me know ahead of time; that way I could have juggled my other bills around!" She knew she needed help in the first place, but she wanted Malcolm to be responsible. I understood. Carmen knew I would do anything in the world for her, anything. Before lending any money, Carmen, Malcolm, Darnell, and I had a verbal understanding that the money was a loan and we would be paid back every dime. Malcolm had just lucked up on a job and made it clear that he would be the one paying us back.

About three weeks later Carmen stopped by asking if she could borrow ten dollars and I gave it to her. I saw that she and Malcolm were together, so I thought it was the perfect time to inquire about when to expect my first payment. I didn't want to act drastically, considering he hadn't been on the job long, but I was getting the impression that he was planning on paying us back upon his own selfish terms, and not to mention, the two of them started become distant and standoffish towards Darnell and I.

Carmen said, "You have to go talk to Malcolm about what he owe you; I ain't got nothin' to do with that." She had everything to do with it, because she's the one who asked for the money, and once I agreed to loan them the money that's when Malcolm decided to come in as her co-signer. I walked out to the car to talk to Malcolm and that n**** handed me a five-dollar bill.

"What the heck do you expect me to do with this?" I said. "This ain't even enough to buy a pack of cigarettes."

Malcolm said, "Well, I ain't tryin' to get you high. I told you I would pay you back; whether I give you two or five dollars a week, I'm paying you back."

"Dang! Can I at least get fifty biweekly, enough to pay a utility bill or stock up on household necessities?"

"I never told you how much I would give you just as long

as I pay the money back. I make minimum wage, and have to pay you back what I can and when I can. That's your business what you do with it as long as I'm paying you back," he replied.

I walked away, not ever mentioning that money to them again. I chalked it up as a loss. One thing I knew about my Father is: He would pay us back more than what we loaned out; the devil would only triumph for so long. The victory was ours! Darnell was pissed when I told him, but never said a word to Malcolm or Carmen on behalf of me, because of the love I had for my sister.

> *Be a lender not a borrower*
> *A leader not a follower.*
> *Joel & Sherese Jordan*

17

Down in the Valley

All who had the lesser seniority on the job were handed pink slips at the end of the day. When it rains it pours of course; count it all joy…thus says the Lord! Darnell was eligible for unemployment, but I wasn't, because I didn't fall within the proper parameters. The following month Section 8 started paying the bulk of the rent, and I started job hunting again, in need of another source of income. I felt this was the time for Carmen and Malcolm to step up to the plate financially, considering our situation. Malcom had only paid us twice, maybe twenty or twenty-five dollars in all. I swear, I literally shouldn't give that much credit, because I'm merely rounding off to the nearest dollar. It was all good, I wasn't going to sweat it, I was determined not to mention that money to them ever again and didn't. Neither did they.

Thank God Darnell and I met Bobby, a bail bondsman. He took turns taking Darnell and me on short road trips bounty hunting. If the criminal was on parole, Bobby took Darnell just in case a situation got out of hand, and he saved the probation violators for me.

My uncle Aaron passed away. My aunt Lynn was a flight attendant and gave me a buddy pass to fly out to Maryland where the funeral was held, and from there I headed straight for Detroit. I needed space and time away, and Diane was missing all of us, including Darnell. I missed Ladondra; it had been a long time since I'd last seen or talked with her, and I wanted to see her, but I had no luck on her whereabouts. I stopped over to Nina's house, and unfortunately she was going through serious hell. It was hard enough losing her brother just a few years ago, but then the Lord called home Nina's pride and joy, her mother. I made my visit to Nina's my last stop in Detroit, before Diane and I hit the road to drive me back South. Nina was so stressed out, she packed her and the kids a week's worth of clothing, and came back with us to Tennessee without asking if she could visit. I knew then, Nina was going through it. Other than the Lord Himself, I was honored to be the one to relieve her of stress and be her comfort zone. She knew she didn't need permission to visit.

I hung out with a few other friends I hadn't saw in some time the night before leaving, and didn't return until the next morning. I made it in enough time to hit the highway. Nina and Diane took turns driving; I wasn't going to make it. I was nervous, having anxiety attacks from not resting all night. Even if I had been rested, the anxiety attacks were a health issue that had been a part of my life for years. The doctors tried putting me on medication, but I chose not to take it. I trusted God would make it better. I didn't need medication running my life. Nina was laughing at me because Diane was talking crap as usual about me and my attacks. "There she goes with that paranoia bull****."

Both Diane and Nina loved the house. Diane hugged Darnell as they cracked a few jokes on each other; I wondered how long that was going to last.

Diane decided to video record the family. She gave Daevon the keys to the van and told him to look in the trunk for the video recorder, but he came back inside claiming he didn't see it. Diane instantly turned from Dr. Jekyll to Mrs. Hyde as usual. "Oh, you better find it, because I put it in there."

Nina was in the kitchen, drunk, frying wing dings, and laughing her heart out. She knew it was about to go down with Diane and Darnell. I just buried my head in the palm of my hands. "Here they go, on the first night!" I looked at Nina with eyes to kill; she always had a bad habit of laughing at all the wrong things, and at the wrong time. "Do you ever take anything serious?" I didn't see anything funny. Diane was always full of trouble, and I didn't need her turning the peace I had in my home into an uproar.

Darnell searched upstairs for the camera. Diane searched downstairs while the both of them yelled and argued back and forth. Nina was way past her alcohol limit, bent over laughing with tears in her eyes, and burning up batches of chicken. The kids were just standing there; it's shameful to say that they were used to the drama between Diane and Darnell. Diane went out to search the trunk herself and found her video camera right where she had placed it. Daevon didn't take the time to look for it; he just opened the trunk, didn't see it lying within his lazy eye vision, so he closed the trunk and came back inside. Luggage and bags were packed in the trunk, and he didn't feel like moving anything. The devil was busy all the way from Detroit to Tennessee. Diane apologized. I was still pissed, so I turned in early while all three drunks hung out all night eating burnt chicken and getting drunker.

Diane and Nina prepared to head back home. I thought about how I actually appreciated that first night's drama because it broke the ice between Diane and Darnell; it actually brought them closer. Nina needed that laughter. Every day that Nina spent with me, something happened that kept her laughing hilariously and up in spirit. I guess that made it all worthwhile. As many years as Diane and Darnell had been bickering, you'd think I'd be used to it, but hell I was traumatized from all that mess coming up in my childhood years. You never knew when to relax with Diane—she had evil ways, and you never knew what she had up her sleeve. Diane was one woman who faithfully lived up to the expectations of her zodiac signs; she was a Pisces. She was all good whenever swimming upstream, and then out the clear blue waters she'd do 180 degree turn around down stream and flake up on you while bringing you down at the same time. Diane always had some form of mental control over me; she kept me in fear of her some kind of way.

I had just returned home from shopping, and Darnell and his buddy were sitting on the front porch. For some reason looking into Darnell's eyes gave me an unsettling feeling in my spirit. I said to myself, "*I'm not going down this road again*". I looked into his eyes, and instantly saw a vision of him relapsing. I could smell our past in the atmosphere.

When his buddy left, I bluntly asked him if he was backsliding again, and unfortunately I couldn't get a straight answer. I wanted to choke the life out of Darnell. God knows I didn't want to leave him, because other than our kids he was the only someone who loved me unconditionally. However, I was determined not to go down that road again. The storm we went through in Florida made me stronger and wiser. I knew that I could survive without Darnell.

I asked Carmen for one dollar and seventy-five cents, and she claimed not to have it. About a half hour later I got a phone call from another source telling me Carmen said, "She got me messed up. I'm not giving her a dime to give to Darnell to get high!" Everybody said she was wrong for feeling that way, after all the help Darnell and I had provided for her and her family. I wanted money to add to what I already had so I could get a drink and drown my sorrows away. That's what I had started doing after having absolutely no one to turn to in Tennessee. Carmen wasn't any different than Darnell's family in Florida. I rarely cried out to Sheila, because I knew Carmen had a jealous heart. If you were close to her, she wanted it to stay that way, and she didn't want you getting close to anyone else she knew. Carmen wanted everybody to herself individually and always had to be the center of attention. Her nieces and I were so close, they called me auntie, but I slowly broke all that up when they told me Carmen said I wasn't their real aunt. Although, they didn't care and they loved me, I started becoming distant over time. I never lost my love for them. I just didn't want to come between Carmen and her family, because biologically... they belonged to her, not me.

I wouldn't hustle money for Darnell when we were already sliding down in the valley on razor blades and alcohol. We had five children, no family in Tennessee to turn to, and again were far from our hometown.

When Darnell was getting high, it was with his own money. I didn't have any income coming in. I was managing his unemployment because that's all we had, and yes, I gave him a few dollars here and there. It was his money. When we were broke, it was because he found money I had hidden; some kind of way Darnell would find it. I used to put money in Ziploc bags and hide it in my plants deep underneath the dirt. The next morning dirt would be piled onto the floor like our puppy had been digging for his bone, but I came to find out Darnell had been training me to talk in my sleep. I was beginning to furiously hate Darnell. Every time he pulled out the driveway to go feed his habit, I would pray hard for God not to bring him back, but to keep him safe. I didn't care about the car. I just wanted peace. I wanted my life back, and was trying to keep hold of my sanity. Things had gotten so bad and out of hand that the furniture company started posting large lime-green stickers all over my front door and garage to embarrass us for not paying our bill. The repo man started prowling around, so eventually we had to file bankruptcy. We had paid too many car notes and furniture bills to just give them up without a fight.

In the meantime, rumors started spreading everywhere. I received a phone call from someone. "Carmen is going around spreading rumors that you and Darnell are pissed off about y'all money because Darnell's on crack." Carmen was dirty. Darnell hadn't relapsed until after we were laid off, and we stopped asking about the money way before then. Carmen was rubbing Darnell's name in the dirt because of her small-frame, built, broke Negro not stepping up to the plate like a man should to support his family. Darnell worked his butt off and provided a roof not only over his family's head, but Carmen's too. She had some nerve! She started keeping the kids away from me, saying there was no telling what was going on in my house. Darnell didn't have any company whatsoever coming by; besides, the one time he and his coworker were sitting on the front porch, he definitely didn't do drugs in front of me or the kids.

I became secluded in my room every day, pouring my heart out in tears, playing Cece Winans' "Alabaster Box" over and over again. I was so stressed out that I immediately made preparations to move back to the "D." I wasn't reliving the past again, with Darnell on drugs and no family to turn to. This time Darnell and I were going our separate ways as soon as we hit the Michigan State lines.

The flashing of red and blue lights woke me up. I got up

to look out the window, and saw two police units at Carmen's house. She called, telling me that someone had broken into her house, trashed it, and only stole a microwave. Carmen said she knew Darnell broke into her house. I told her if she felt that way then give the police his name and identity and send them over here. I would take it from there. Carmen never spoke a word to the cops about Darnell, why?

A few hours later Darnell pulled into the driveway, and I met him at the front door, asking him if broke into Carmen's house, but he never responded. He gave himself away by not responding; he was completely out of order. I also wondered why he only took the microwave and didn't clean house, especially considering he was a drug addict. I mean, who does that? "America's Dumbest Criminal!" is what I thought.

The next day I saw Sheila. "Baby, you know why Darnell did that, don't you? I told you he was overprotective over you. He sees how your sister's been mistreating you and watching you cry all through the day and night, stressing yourself, and it affected him. He had no intentions of stealing anything; that's why he only took the microwave. He wanted Carmen and Malcom to know that it was him who did it and why he did it."

I had forgotten all about Sheila mentioning how Darnell would go to the ends of the world if someone hurt me. However, at the end of the day Carmen was still my sister and I loved her. I felt really bad and extremely embarrassed. I still couldn't understand why Carmen didn't tell the police, but she didn't. Eventually everything went back to normal.

The police showed up on my doorstep at 6:00 a.m., right when it was time to wake the children for school. Darnell had got hold of my checkbook and wrote a hundred-dollar check to himself. The check bounced. The officer allowed me to get the kids off to school; he didn't want them seeing me get arrested. He also made me call my bondsman so he could meet me down at the station and bail me out before handcuffing me and locking me in a cell; the cops were very compassionate in Tennessee.

I found out Darnell had wrote so many outstanding checks that I was being arrested at least twice a week. The first time Carmen went nuts, but I didn't really care. I was numb to everybody, I felt I had no one to turn to; I was in this mess alone.

The job called Darnell and me back to work, but both for the afternoon shift. I was indecisive of whether I should take on the job or if Darnell should. If I went back that meant more income, but Darnell would've been unstable watching the kids. He was out in the streets so much getting high, and I didn't have anyone else. If he went back to work, I stood a chance of him not being consistent with going to work because of his drug habit; I was baffled. However, when all was said and done, I told him to go back to work, but he started going in late or not going at all just as I expected. I went up to the job and spoke with the supervisor about Darnell's habit because the job offered an in-house drug rehab program for any employee in need. I couldn't believe Darnell signed up for help. However, that only lasted two weeks and he ended up losing the job all together!

Officer Clemens was a good friend of mine; he patrolled our neighborhood. My last time going to jail, I didn't have a bond. I had to cash out five hundred to be released. Officer Clemens happened to be patrolling at the time Carmen was walking up the street. She told him what happened, and he didn't hesitate to give her fifty dollars to help me out, and I really appreciated that. My bail bondsman couldn't help as much as he wanted this time because I had to pay five hundred cash, but he did loan a hundred dollars. The car had broken down, so Darnell rode the bike to the pawn shop with our computer sitting on the handlebars. They gave him six hundred dollars and then placed the computer with the rest of our household items that was sitting on shelves or lying around on the floor collecting dust.

Driving back to Detroit, I reminisced about my living experience in Tennessee compared to Florida. I loved Tennessee— there was definitely no comparison. Tennessee would always be my number one southern state!

We wondered how the heck we were to move back home with the vehicle broken down. We really didn't have the expenses to rent a vehicle; we only had enough to rent a moving truck. We hadn't nearly as much money as we had when moving south. I had to call Diane and ask if she would drive down to help us get back to Detroit; I knew she had been missing Daevon and figured since she had a pleasant stay when she visited with us, she wouldn't mind driving south again.

Diane decided to bring my grandmother along to see how well I was living. Yeah, right, if they only knew. I didn't mentioned the move to Carmen, I only told her mother. My plan was to just get ghost, considering Darnell and her were the main reasons for my relocating back home. I didn't want to take Darnell back to the "D,". I appreciated Darnell. Diane was troubled water, and he was my bridge to cross over, so getting him back to the city was the least I could do. Darnell put me and his family through a lot, but that didn't mean he didn't love us genuinely. Darnell was sick; he had an addiction. I didn't want to leave him in a foreign land where he had no family. I knew if I stayed south I would not have been able to get rid of him. I had to get him back to the city where he had family, knew people and how to hustle so he could provide for himself and his habit some kind of way.

The news spread quickly about my moving back north and it resulted in everybody being sad. We were the life of the block. After I made my decision to move, everybody else on the block decided they wanted to move as well, starting with my next-door neighbor Angie; she ended up moving before me. Next, Carmen wanted to move back to the city and so did Sheila, but I really didn't want Carmen tagging along. I didn't turn my back on either of them, because I was never the type of woman to hold grudges, and anyway it wasn't like we were going to share the same house once we moved.

When the day came for us to move, Darnell packed all three houses on one truck. What a hell-hole mess that was, and he acted a butthole the entire time. Darnell knew he was about to hit rock-bottom without me.

The morning of the move Diane grew impatient, ready to leave. She took my three oldest boys and Carmen's family and bailed out; she didn't bother waiting on the rest of my household so we could all ride back together. The rental company kept harassing Darnell and me about Carmen running off with their merchandise, demanding us to let them search the truck, but we didn't. We were left with Carmen's troubled baggage and ours too. We had trouble loading our broken-down car on the bed of the truck. We were left with a huge mess while Carmen and Sheila rode ahead of us without a concern in the world.

Once we made it back to the city, we stopped over to Carmen's cousin's house to unload her and Sheila's belongings, and once again Darnell started acting like a butthole. Our separating was dawning on him, and he knew it was too late because I kept warning him. We were all standing outside while Darnell and the puppy were in the truck. Carmen was standing by the driver's side and Darnell asked her to hold our puppy for a moment. He then pulled off with the truck like a bat out of hell. Some of our things went flying off into the street. Carmen looked down at the puppy, as Sheila started chasing the truck down the street, screaming, "THAT'S ALL THE STUFF I HAVE TO MY NAME, PLEASE DARNELL! WAAIIT!" I buried my head in the palm of my hands. Even though he was angry, I knew he was coming back, but still, it was beyond embarrassing.

Twenty minutes later he pulled up and everything on the truck was in shambles due to his reckless driving. At that moment it wasn't funny, but as time went by, Carmen and Sheila laughed tears from their eyes. I still didn't think it was funny. The most hilarious to them was him handing the puppy to Carmen, and then pulling off like he did; we all thought his intentions were to help unload their belongings.

Diane rekindled her fire with an old flame from back in the day. Rick was a pedophile and an alcoholic. He used to hang out with me and Nina's family when we were kids. Rick was drunk every time he came around. He always tried to get me and Nina alone and bribe us into allowing him to stick his hands down our shirt. He always had a five- or ten-dollar bill folded tightly in the palm of his hands, ready to stick it down in our bra and get his rocks off. "I'll pay you every time I stick my hand in; how much ya wanna make?" I see that day so clear. How gross! Nina and I weren't even teenagers. Rick didn't care though; he would even offer to pay me five dollars for every kiss I gave him. Nina and I would look at him in disgust every time. We told our parents, but I can't say if they really took it to heart; being a pedophile wasn't a common issue back then. I only remember them talking about him like the dog he was, because he flirted with darn near every woman in his eyesight. If our parents did do something about it you sure as heck couldn't tell, because he continued to come around for years. You know, I never stopped and actually thought why Diane allowed him around me, knowing I had been sexually abused repetitiously. Nor did I take the time to think why she would rekindle a relationship with him twenty years later. My brain just didn't function that way, and apparently neither did Diane's.

Rick allowed me and my children to stay with them for one month rent free. I didn't want to, but I had no choice considering the drastic move I made from Tennessee. Even though Rick seemed a changed man all except for his drinking habit, I still kept my eyes on him. My daughter Dejah was just an infant, but I didn't care. I didn't put anything past anybody; Dejah was my only daughter. I was extremely protective over her.

I had been under a tremendous amount of stress dealing with Darnell, who wouldn't leave me alone. Instead of turning in the moving truck, he parked it down the street from where I was living. He couldn't let go; he kept using excuses that he didn't have anywhere to go when he knew good and well he could have lived with his dad. He just wanted to play on my emotions by sleeping in the truck; he thought I would feel sorry for him. If I continued allowing us to live together, we would've all been sleeping in that truck. I was better off feeling sorry for him alone than feeling sorry for us all.

18

22 Weeks Too Long

Carmen and I went to look at a house she'd found for rent. The neighborhood wasn't bad, befitting enough for the kids and me to live in for starters, but deep down in my spirit I wasn't feeling it. Carmen was only attracted to the plush gray carpeting throughout the main floor. She and the landlord talked me into it, so I took it. I couldn't afford waiting until the last minute, as my month was almost up living with Rick and Diane.

I saw Gary on the block; I missed him so much. He was close to my sons because he had been around them since they were in the belly. He kept them intact during their upcoming years and I really wanted him to move in and help me keep the boys together since Darnell and I were separating. Now was the time for a male figure to be in their lives since they were becoming young men. I felt Gary was the best candidate as he and the boys were already close; they confided in him.

I met Melvin on a visit with Arielle and my godchildren. She lived with her man Jaron. I liked him because he was a hard worker, a homeowner, and cool people. Melvin was his brother and he was cool too. He was a skinny dude and always had on his work uniform. Melvin wasn't my taste in a man, but what attracted me was his ambition getting up every Sunday and all suited up for church. Also, it was a relief from the stressed relationship I'd just got out of, and I was hoping Melvin was my contented outlet. I had been through so much that I assumed hooking up with Melvin would take my mind away from the fresh past.

Melvin and I became closely acquainted. He let me drive him to work so I could keep his car and get situated back in the city. I took advantage of going job hunting and transporting the kids back and forth to school. One main attribute that stood out with Melvin was his relationship with his children. He had two daughters and a son; Melvin Jr., Jackie, and Asia. They were all by the same mother, and I really respected him for that. The kids' teachers knew Melvin very well. He attended every parent/teacher conference meeting and participated in some of the school activities and programs. He introduced me to his family, and they were all close, attending the same church, and were good for family gatherings. The first time meeting Melvin's kids, he introduced me to their mother Pam and her family. I could tell she and the family loved Melvin because he was there for his children; they were cool people.

I couldn't believe Diane actually liked Melvin. I think she marveled at the fact that he attended church every Sunday and came by for dinner afterward all suited up. He also carried a gun but wasn't a thug at all; he claimed he believed in self-preservation. Diane really liked that because she kept one too. I wasn't too fond of it!

Melvin drove the moving truck, because Gary and I knew nothing about driving a stick-shift. I drove with two feet but couldn't handle a stick-shift; weird! Melvin knew how to drive anything on wheels, even tractor trailers.

I got my old job back working at the phone company, because I left on good standards when relocating to Tennessee. I registered all the kids in school. I had to spend the day with Dejah in kindergarten. Every day I had to ease my way out by telling her I was going to bring her a Happy Meal; it worked every time. Please believe by the end of the day, she and lil' Darnell were expecting those Happy Meals.

Gary and Melvin were cool. Melvin also gelled well with the kids, and all of our kids became really close. Darnell and I had only been separated a few months and already I had allowed Melvin to move in. I knew I was moving way too fast, but I just couldn't stand the thought of being alone. I never could. If me and a man weren't living together it was family and close friends. The fruit didn't fall far from the tree.

Melvin's kids came over every weekend, and when summer arrived they stayed with us the entire time. Gary lived with us too—that was the norm. Wherever we moved in the city Gary was sure to come.

Melvin was laid off, not having enough seniority and only being employed with the company less than a year. Unfortunately, he was denied unemployment because he didn't fall within the required quarters—same thing that happened with me. He started looking for another job, but in between time he kept the entire house clean, including the kids' rooms. Laundry was washed, dried, folded, and placed properly in the dresser drawers, and some ironed and neatly hung on hangers. Melvin was a good cook; it felt good coming home to a clean house, and meals prepared too. I trusted my judgment especially with Gary living with us. I know I wouldn't have allowed Melvin to stay at the house being the only adult considering it had only been a few months. I trained myself not to get too relaxed and spoiled, because I preferred paychecks, not housekeeping.

Darnell eventually turned in the moving truck and went over to his dad's to live. He wanted to keep our puppy Keke, because it gave him that sense of family security as if, he still had an everyday connection with us. The kids spent the weekends with him whenever he requested for them. However, that didn't last after having a gunfight with his dad's girlfriend's brother. I stopped the kids from visiting, and brought Keke with us to live.

The brother was no longer allowed over, but I still waited a while before allowing the kids back over just to make sure the guy was officially gone.

Melvin and the kids were wrestling one day, and Keke wanted in on some action as always. Melvin took offense. I couldn't understand why, because Keke was a purse-size puppy that couldn't bite a finger if she tried. Melvin rolled up a newspaper and spanked her. "That dog ain't gone be growlin' at me." I had a talk with Melvin away from the kids, and tried hard to shake it off. I didn't want our relationship to go downhill because of one incident, even though I took serious offense to it. Melvin just didn't know Keke the way we knew her, so I thought we could work on that, considering it being so minor.

Early Saturday afternoon the kids were outdoors playing. I headed toward the back door to let in the fresh-air breeze, but noticed no Keke. She wasn't playing with the kids as she usually did. Keke had disappeared, including the leash. The kids never inquired about her. I asked them, but they didn't know; strange. I knew Gary didn't know, because he'd spent the night out. I asked Melvin, but he claimed not to know, with a look of dismay plastered on his face.

I was deeply saddened; my kids thought she ran away. I

tried viewing the situation from every angle. Keke wasn't used to being in the city or being on a leash. Also, the transition from Darnell's to our house could have put a strain on her. However, after analyzing everything, my spirit led me to believe she didn't run away. I rested my head on the storm door, closed my saturated eyes, and went into deep memory. Remembering back in Tennessee when the kids waited on the school bus, Keke was always standing right there with them. Every time the bus pulled off the block, she ran behind until it turned onto the main street; then she'd just sit there until the bus was out of her sight. When afternoon hit she would leave the house five minutes early, sitting in the exact same spot where the bus picked up the kids because she knew they were on their way. For breakfast, lunch, and dinner she always nudged her doggy bowl with her nose, pushing it under the table so she could eat with the family.

I know Keke didn't run away; she was too happy, too close to us. I know Melvin had something to do with her disappearance, but I had no proof. I began keeping my eyes on Melvin.

The Christmas holiday rolled around, and Darnell asked if he could spend some time with the kids, so I dropped them off. When it came time for them to come home, Melvin and I went to pick them up and Darnell had been drinking and decided to act a fool. He told me I couldn't get the kids unless we all spent some family time together. He was pissed about our puppy; I understood that, but our relationship had been done and was no more. Melvin heard the argument through the car window, so he got out and walked up to the front porch to confront Darnell. I don't remember who swung the first punch, but the rumbling began. Darnell stepped back in the house and within seconds came back out with a hammer and starting swinging on Melvin. I begged Darnell to stop; Melvin had so many lumps on his head he looked like Tom the cat after a beat-down from Jerry.

The next day Diane saw Melvin's head and fell out laughing so hard she choked. Melvin couldn't help but laugh too, because she was cracking jokes. I had a straight face. I knew it was payback for Melvin after taking over the family, and leaving Darnell destitute, and for Keke's disappearance.

Later that evening Darnell called me and said Melvin drove by and fired two shots through their window. Oh my God, it was time to get rid of him, and I knew I was going to have to play it smart. At first, I couldn't understand why Darnell didn't call the police, but he told me Melvin shot towards the top of the window. Their house had tall windows, so you would have to be almost seven feet tall to get hit by the bullet. Melvin knew what he was doing. Darnell knew Melvin was only trying to scare him, but he wasn't scared. I planned on talking to Gary, but he was never there. I guess since I had Melvin, he didn't want to feel like he was in the way, but he wasn't. I loved having Gary around.

My godchildren came over with plans of spending the night; they too, were close to Melvin's kids. Everything was cool until it was time for the kids to get ready for bed. They cleaned their faces, brushed their teeth, and then began to say their bedtime prayers. Out of nowhere Melvin furiously yelled out to his kids, "Y'all better not say no damn prayers take y'all a**** to sleep. Y'all don't know sh** about no damn prayers!" I was a little shocked at Melvin considering his family's tradition; they were church going folk. I didn't say a word though, because they were his children. I made sure mine and Arielle's kids continued to pray, because that's how we raised ours. He continued yelling, "Arielle's kids ain't spending the night; send their a**** home in a cab!" My oldest goddaughter wasn't even ten years of age and even if she was they weren't going anywhere.

Heck, I thought, let him and his kids hop in a cab and get out! But I was tongue-careful. Melvin was a ticking time bomb with a gun on his side. He didn't go anywhere and he watched everything! I mean this man changed with the wind. Melvin started watching my every move and slept with one eye open. My every move was peacefully and carefully done.

I was very careful how I dropped hints concerning my plans to cease the relationship. Melvin wore that gun on his side like it was a belt around his waist; it went everywhere he went. I had to consider the consequences of my kids being in danger if Melvin and I were to fall out. After the Darnell situation I didn't know what he thought of us or where his head was. I was in fear!

The other issue I had with Melvin and his youngest daughter Asia was the jealousy toward the relationship I had with my goddaughters. Melvin just wanted our kids in the picture, and wanted me to forget about my godchildren. I would never put anybody else's children over them. I vowed to be their godmother even living in heaven, and that's what I intended to do. I love them so much. They've been under my wing since in the belly, and I'm supposed to turn my back on them for some man and his kids? Never! Asia was so envious of Dejah, because she wanted to be my number one child. I showed all of the children equal love and they were all happy, but she wanted that extra mile—something I wasn't going to give her. I treated all of them equal and wasn't going to give Asia better treatment over my only daughter.

Arielle and Jaron came by to pick up the girls. In order to keep the peace, I didn't even mention what happened the night before; I knew my godchildren were going to tell it all. All the kids were upstairs playing except my youngest goddaughter, Keela. Not even two hours later Jaron and Melvin started arguing; Jaron was drunk. They were jealous of each other, and it always related back to their mother favoring one son over the other. Jaron pulled his gun out and Melvin charged at him before he could pull the trigger that was aimed at him. Jaron was also one to carry a gun, but only when he was out not sitting in his house 24/7 like Melvin. They were fighting directly in front of Arielle while she was holding baby Keela, and the gun was going off, shooting in all directions. Arielle was screaming for me to grab Keela. She should've been trying to hover over Keela and/or dropping to the floor for some kind of safety. My focus was on the kids who were trying to come down the stairs, because of all the commotion they may have heard. The gun was pointed in their direction at that very moment. I yelled for them to go back upstairs as I headed in their direction with my arms wrapped around my head as a shield of protection. By the time the kids headed back up and I redirected my mind on the baby, Melvin and Jaron had stopped fighting. Thank God nobody was hurt.

After everybody left Melvin apologized repeatedly for his brother's actions, and then afterwards he left, in need of some air. An hour later Jaron and Arielle phoned me about Melvin doing a drive-by at their house, shooting the brick of the house only. Again, he called himself instilling fear in Jaron, but what if the bullet strayed and went through the window? I had to get away from Melvin…quick!

Once I hung up, Melvin walked through the door. "I couldn't let him disrespect us like that, so I went over there and shot. I wasn't trying to hurt anybody, just scare them, because we had kids over here, and that n**** crazy!" Melvin said. They were both crazy! My, my, my, I had no idea what I had gotten myself caught up in. The quicker I tried to end the relationship, the more intense situations started taking place.

Gary came home three or four days later after hearing gossip. He didn't care for Melvin much at all after seeing who he really was. Melvin was intimidated by Gary and wanted him to leave. They hadn't fallen out or anything; Melvin just wanted full control and didn't want Gary in the way, because he knew how close we were. Gary watched his back as he walked out the door; Melvin had changed rapidly. As Gary was walking up the street with his bags, I started crying intensely which made Melvin furious, so furious that he grabbed my rifle and pointed it straight toward Gary's back while he was walking; Gary didn't even know it. Melvin said, "If you keep cryin' over this n****, I'ma blow his motha efn back out!" Immediately I dried my tears. I didn't want to make any sudden moves and definitely didn't want Gary to hear us. I believed if Gary turned around and looked back Melvin would've shot him. Or he would've come back with his boys, and that could've put me and the kids in even more danger, because we were right there in the house with Melvin's crazy self.

I should have been more observant when Melvin's sister told me the reason why the family didn't get too close to me. Melvin's relationships never lasted more than five months except with his ex-wife, and that's because she was crazy too. And according to Melvin and a few of his family members she was a mentally sick woman. Melvin was the only one who would put up with her and vice versa.

I sent the kids away with their dad for the weekend so I could put a master plan together. I told them not to tell their dad what transpired. Melvin's kids were back at home as the school year had started back. I had to cook at a cabaret Carmen's people were giving. I so needed a different atmosphere in order to clear my head and figure out a way to get rid of Melvin. I was glad Melvin didn't come to the cabaret, because Jaron and

Arielle were there and the beef wasn't over.

After the party ended the security guard came into the kitchen alarming the cooks about a guy outside with a BB gun talking crazy. Then out of the blue Jaron started his bull-crap as usual. He was standing on the table drunk and ready to fight for nothing. Meanwhile, I was in the kitchen cleaning up as Melvin walked in angrily, wondering how much longer I would be. "About forty-five minutes, and what's wrong with you?" He just walked out without answering me. Come to find out it was him outside with the BB gun. He was on some jealous-junk, needing a reason to start drama. He wanted to catch me with some man, but he knew I wasn't like that. Melvin wasn't used to peace in his life or in his relationships. He had low self-esteem because he never had a woman of my class.

Once we reached home I said a prayer for peace and stayed up through the night. There were only a few hours until sunrise; something was going to have to shake immediately! I sat there thinking about all I had done for his kids, and how I stayed by his side when he was broke. Maybe that was part of his insecurities; me taking care of the bills and his kids while he was housewife'n. Melvin stayed up all night too, searching for his gun that he couldn't find. He never told me he lost it, because he knew I would be in control then. Now I understand why he started using my rifle.

I finally stood up to Melvin; I let him have it until he slammed me to the floor so hard he caused my shoulder-blade to crack. I then balled up in excruciating pain, unable to move my arm. The only thing that held my arm and shoulder together was the meat and skin attached. He then decided to help me back on my feet and I told him right then and there in the most polite and respectful way, "Get out!" Melvin went straight to the closet and pulled out my rifle that I had obviously forgotten about just that darn quick. He aimed at my head in all attempts of pulling the trigger. I grabbed the rifle in quick reflex. I used my left hand because my right side was out of socket and the pain was beyond excruciating. I pleaded for my life—I had no strength with the use of one arm. Melvin calmed down and out the blue, he asked if I wanted something to eat. He demanded that it be something quick, because he didn't feel like cooking. That n**** was past unstable! I wasn't surprised at his comment at all, and definitely didn't want him cooking me anything. I was speechless! Me and my decisions! All I wanted was to be free from Darnell and I ended up in an even worst situation.

While waiting for a doctor, a mad nurse came walking in the room looking like Madea. She made Melvin step out of the room. She didn't even bother asking what happened; she got straight to the point. "Did he do it?" I said yes and the police were there in less than five minutes, but Melvin was gone in three. I called myself allowing Melvin to take me to the hospital, because I knew once I told the doctor what happened they were sending for the authorities without Melvin knowing. Apparently, his irritating demonic self was eavesdropping. It was over for Melvin! When I was released Diane drove to the hospital to pick me up, and she was extremely upset.

Gary was at the house waiting on Melvin in the backyard. When Melvin pulled up in my car, the window was rolled down. He was on his cell phone trying to reach his lawyer, but Gary snatched the phone and cracked Melvin upside the head with it. Gary beat Melvin down as he pleaded for his life, trying to take off in my car. Melvin jumped out of the car and ran to the neighbor's house crying and begging for them to call 911. The police arrived and took the "World's Dumbest Criminal" straight to jail. The devil always falls down in the hole he digs for someone else!

A few months later Melvin was ambushed! He was shot up so bad that his arm was barely hanging on to his shoulder...just like mine. Melvin was dangerous to himself, his children, and others. He was insanely unstable. He shot at Darnell's father house, Arielle and Jaron's house, tried to blow my head off, and dislocated my arm from my shoulder. Melvin had it coming!

Melvin Jr. came by to say hello. He told me some terrible news! Melvin shot Keke with the BB gun in his son's presence and then tossed her in a trash bag and threw her in a Dumpster off of Mack Ave. I was outraged!

The horrific things Melvin did, said, and displayed to his children, may have negatively impacted their future, and especially his son. It's so sad to say that Melvin didn't play much of a positive role in his son's life. He was too busy showing him how to shoot, take guns apart, and put them back together again.

I found out that Melvin was never laid-off his job, he quit. His stepbrother told me Melvin was bragging about living off of me because I made enough money for a two-man job. I didn't give Melvin money or provide clothes or shoes for him. Every now and then I bought him a can of beer or two, and sometimes a pack of cigarettes. Melvin wasn't even worth a dollar shot of liquor or one loose cigarette, but I helped him out anyway. I was providing well over enough for his three children and he couldn't even stand that. I guess that was money he felt I could have spent on him. I wasn't in the business of paying a man I was in a relationship with who was living with me jobless and rent-free. Melvin was eating free with the use of water, lights and gas; that was already too much!

22 weeks wasted on a blockhead in a Sunday suit. Shoulda rebuked him Saturday!

A TOUCH BEFORE INSANITY

Discipline your children while there is hope.
Otherwise you will ruin their lives.
Proverbs 19:18

19

Tainted Love

Gary's boy Keith lived a few houses down and every day he came by, because he and Gary had become very close friends. On this particular day I went off on Keith because he went into the kitchen and grabbed a glass of water after I'd just finished scrubbing and cleaning. He looked at me without saying a word, undressing me with his eyes, and I have to admit, it turned me on sexually.

The next morning I told Gary I wanted to have a one-night stand with Keith.

"Keith? Said Gary."

I looked at him in bewilderment, wondering if there was something deep and dark I needed to know about Keith. I knew he lived with his baby-mama, but according to Keith, Gary, and talk on the block, their relationship had long perished before I moved in the hood. They also said his baby mama would recite that famous old quote, "You leave me, you leave family". From my understanding, based on words that came from Keith's lips, he was only in the relationship for the sake of the child, but it was only pushing him away and causing him to re-act rebelliously. I just assumed Gary was shocked at the idea of me even considering a hood negro like Keith. After two failed relationships of one, Darnell and his serious drug and alcohol addiction, and Melvin, who turned out to be the sheep in wolf's clothing, I just needed to be free for just a minute. But a woman of my character considering a guy like Keith, even if it was a one-night stand, was beyond Gary's understanding.

"Out of all my boys, I never pictured a woman of your character having an interest whatsoever in a nigga like Keith!"

Plus Keith was only twenty-two and I was thirty-three, but I didn't care. I looked at it as contingency it wasn't like I was fifty. I could bring the man out in him, starting with his spirituality, teaching him how to pray regularly and converse with God. Other than that, Keith had that STS (street thug swag) that turned me on, and it'd been over a year since I'd been sexed.

Eventually Keith and I hooked up, but that one night led to another after another and so on. The more I had sex with him, the more tainted I became. That can be dangerous! After a few months of messing around with Keith, I literally asked God to bless me with him. I felt like a man of God can't be nothing but good to a woman. This is what I wanted from Keith; you can't possibly go wrong if God is in the midst.

The more I became tainted, the more I had to pray; I never experienced such a feeling. It was all so foreign to me. It was like trying to distinguish the difference between being in love or being under a curse. I was perplexed. I couldn't begin to explain what had erratically come over me. I could tell that Keith was falling in love too. Of course, being a woman, I outwardly expressed my emotions more so than he . I'd literally get sick to the stomach if three days went by without me seeing him.

I even tested my emotions by trying to let go of him and couldn't. That wouldn't have stopped Keith, because he was the type of guy who would climb through my window, even if I locked it. He would've gotten to me some way, somehow! If being in love felt like that, I didn't want it. It was the strangest feeling in the world.

Although Keith and Deena's relationship was beyond shambles, I still felt guilty. The average woman who falls in love with a man who's already in another relationship is typically relentless. It's competition for a woman, because sometimes we allow these types of situations to validate our beauty and power. On some occasions this can lead to a dangerously jealous spirit if the situation doesn't play out as we expect it to. When we don't become that #1 woman, and the man insists on playing with both, that's when everything hits the fan.

Things had gotten haywire and out of control within the few months Keith and I were together. There was always gossip going on; it was like Keith and I were celebrities living in the hood. I couldn't understand out of all the relationships going on in the hood, good or bad, why was ours so significant. I had to kneel down to God and beg him to control my emotions, to control everything that was going on around me; it felt like a curse had come upon me, and I couldn't control it I couldn't escape it. In the beginning I asked God to bless me with Keith and I would convert his life over to Christ; maybe I should have been careful of what I asked for, because the more I prayed for God to control my emotions, the more intense my feelings became and the more I felt deviant. I couldn't understand it for the life of me.

As for Keith, he definitely wasn't trying to end the relationship, but he wasn't going through the motion in the same way as me. I expressed my feelings to Gary first. I didn't want to tell Keith anything that would give him any more power than it seemed like he already had. I needed to figure it out first; I didn't want him to take advantage of my feeling vulnerable. Although Keith had fallen in love with me, he still had the best of both worlds; he had a family to go home to whenever he wanted and me as a sidekick...whenever he wanted me. All I had were my erratic, intense emotions to deal with, which had already become too overwhelming for me to deal with.

Keith didn't talk a lot, he kicked it with his boys, but when it came to his relationships, he kept quiet. He didn't trust people. Keith being so mysterious to me is what kept my feelings tucked away. He was the type that only let you in so much; you had to figure him out every now and then. As crazy as this may sound, his mysterious personality was one of his greatest attributes that turned me on.

Waking up feeling woozy from dreaming, I was swimming under water with the fish, had me running straight to the bathroom. I was aware of the possibilities because the condoms only lasted for so long; the typical relationship. I didn't bother calling Keith to tell him that there was a possibility I could be pregnant. I knew I would see him before the end of the day. If I couldn't reach him on his cell, I could reach him at his house, but that was something I never did. I never considered that as an option, ever.

Later that afternoon Keith came by and I got straight to the point; however, I didn't tell him that the pregnancy was definite because I hadn't taken a pregnancy test. I wasn't surprised at all about his reaction. He had a look in his eyes that read "New life, new destiny." He needed so desperately to get out of the relationship with Deena, because he felt smothered and trapped. He was determined to bring his baby-mama down the street so we could all finally have an intervention. She was aware of our relationship; she just never saw us in action, I guess. She only went by what she heard.

I remember once standing in my backyard, Keith's boy pulled up with Deena, who parked in the middle of the street right in front of my driveway. Keith's boy walked to the back-yard and said, "If Keith's in the house tell'm don't come out or Deena gone bust at his a**." Keith had been long gone earlier that morning. I continued doing what I was doing and let her sit out there when I could've called the police and caused her to catch a case, but I didn't. As far as I was concerned, I wasn't worried about her or her gun; I don't know why, I just wasn't.

However, Keith bringing Deena into a situation before confirmation of my being pregnant was beyond me. Keith de-cided to bring her down the street late night, anyway. I don't think he really cared if I was pregnant or not. I believe it was his cue to get out of the relationship with her. I sat on the passenger side, not feeling any negative energy coming from her. Keith sat in the backseat. Deena got straight to the point. "How long have you and Keith been messing around and are you pregnant?" I told her the truth, but that I hadn't taken a pregnancy test nor had I been to the doctor. I guess my answer was soothing for the moment, because she skipped on to the last question. "Do you love him?"

I held my head down in dismay as I replied, "Yes."

Keith was sitting in the backseat and she looked at him through the rearview mirror and repeated the same question and he immediately said yes, but then the ultimate question was popped.

"Well, who do you love more?"

He didn't respond, but the look in his eyes gave us the im-pression that he didn't want to hurt her any more than he al-ready had. Keith loved her, but not the way she wanted him to. You know how it is when you fall in love again. Especially already being in another relationship, we tend to be confused, our mind becomes cloudy, everything's up in the air. Just when I thought the intervention was over, she went ballistic and screamed out in pain and agony, "WHAT AM I SUPPOSE TO DO?"

I could actually feel her pain, oh God, and I began to ask myself the same question. Keith then stepped out of the car and walked across the field; he was grief-stricken. I had the nerve to try to calm her down by sincerely showing how apologetic I was, knowing I was in love with her man. I didn't know what else to do. I wasn't like some women who didn't care about having an affair with somebody else's man. Usually if a woman falls in love with a guy who's already in a relationship, she doesn't give a darn about his woman crying, because she feels like "Better her than me." Some women use every weapon they were born with to keep the man they love. I also reiterated to Deena that I wasn't sure if I was pregnant. She didn't want to talk anymore; she was emotionally broken down, full of anxiety. I felt extremely horrible. There was nothing I could have said or done to make her feel better. Looking at her reaction I knew Deena would never forget that night. Keith and I had cut her deeply. I knew eventually she would heal and get over it, but the scar would forever be there.

Keith came back to the car and they went home; fifteen minutes later he came back looking as if he had lost the best thing that ever happened to him. Deena and the kids were packing to leave for Muskegon, Michigan. As much as I was in love with Keith, I sincerely encouraged him to go with his family, but he didn't want to. *"I didn't want to hurt her; I never had any intentions on having a relationship or settling down with her. I'm not happy, we don't get along, and she knows how I feel.*

This is something we've been going through for years, but I didn't know how to leave without hurting her and my son. I'm just not happy." After all he said, I was still persistent about him leaving with his family, because I felt guilty. Keith said repeatedly, *"The relationship will never work, it never really has. I only stayed with her because of my mama. When I first told her Deena was pregnant, she told me I might as well stick it out as a family, and I tried, but I just can't do it. I wanna be there for my son, but I don't wanna be with Deena."*

A week had gone by since Deena left, and no matter the length of time or distance between Keith and his son, I knew refraining cold turkey would be difficult; this was a whole new footage for him. He said he and Deena had break-ups before, but he would only leave for a few days. Keith's priority was his only son. Keith said he held his son every night at bedtime, sleeping under the same quilt, while Deena slept under her own quilt. Deena moving out of her own house was completely out the box according to Keith. Through all that suddenly transpired, I tried my best to keep an open mind for the protection of my heart, because I knew there was a strong possibility they would end up back together again.

I took the pregnancy test, following the directions, and had my back turned waiting for the results. Negative! The only thing that trampled through my mind was "He's going to think I tried to trap him!" Even though I did tell him and Deena up front that my pregnancy wasn't confirmed, I was just feeling the symptoms, I still felt like the scheming whore that I really wasn't. I mean the entire situation was already foul, and now this. Deena was probably going to think that I was intentionally trying to hurt her, I but wasn't.

When Keith came by I led him straight to the backyard in need of inhaling fresh air to exhale the results. *"I took the pregnancy test and it was negative. I hope that you're not upset, because I never confirmed that I was definitely pregnant. I also told Deena the same thing the night you left us alone in the car; however, I still do apologize."*

He looked at me. *"I already knew you weren't pregnant."*

I asked him why he brought Deena to my house, but he didn't respond. He just had a deserted look on his face.

Two days later Keith did just as I expected; told me he missed his son and was going to Muskegon to be with him. Instantly I got sick, and not only in the stomach, but emotionally and mentally. I felt just like Deena did the night she officially found out about Keith and me. I got stabbed by my own boomerang. Keith kept telling me he was coming back, but that went through one ear and out the other; all I could do was cry in pain, because at that point I was deeply wounded. I deserved every bit of it.

After he left I was emotionally broken down, and the neighbors across the street came by to sit with me. Nisha was bisexual and Stilts was her cousin; they lived on the block long before me and knew everybody. Both of them tried consoling me and telling me not to cry or worry, he would be back, but again it all went through one ear and out the other. The curse was growing enormously, the weaker I felt the more powerful the curse became, and I began feeling more sick than love itself. I knew that being in love wasn't supposed to feel that way; nothing made sense to me. All I could do was keep praying and keep the faith and pleading with God to please heal me, because I just didn't feel right. There was something about Keith's aura that was toxically contagious. Keith had tainted love.

I couldn't go to work for three consecutive days. Every time I got out of bed my stomach instantly dropped and buckled up; I was severely sick. I couldn't get any sleep at night. I could only lie there and hold my daughter and pray hard until the early dawn. Before she would awake I would get up and kneel down on my knees, crying and praying more. I was scared. I didn't know what was happening to me, especially when it seemed like God had taken his hands off of me. I felt so alone and lost, I didn't know whether I was coming or going.

The fourth day I finally pulled myself together enough to go to work, because I still had to live and provide for my children and I definitely didn't want them seeing what I was going through.

After a few hours of working, I saw Keith walk in. I guess he and Deena had come to the city to visit. Keith walked right past me without saying one word to me; wow! Maybe he was afraid Deena would creep up behind him in the store or send one of her sons in to spy on him. Deena was on Keith like a crack-head on crack. Keith always did act as if he feared her, as if she had power over him to the point if things didn't go her way she had the power to bring him down. Deena had an invisible tether locked on Keith's ankle; she was on him, hard. They had a strange relationship, but looking at what I was going through since I'd been dating him, I would honestly have to say maybe it was Keith himself. He was poison!

The next day after somehow making a way out of Deena's presence, Keith told me he was coming back, but still, never said when. As hard as it was ignoring Keith, I didn't respond. I had to pull myself together some way, somehow.

Gary came strolling up the block fried, walking slanted to the side like he needed a V8. We kicked it for a while. I told him what was going on and it did nothing but upset him. Gary knew Keith was not my type because he was a street n****, and here I was this sweet, honest, naïve, and gullible child. Gary knew I wasn't about that life!

Mr. Greens came over just as we had finished talking; he was known for that name, because he had that good green. He began telling us one of his all-time famous stories.

"I was hanging out wit' my boy, drunk as hell, drivin' up Vandyke Avenue and smacked the back of dis' n****'s car. I was mad as hell, because I was drivin' my mama's s***. I jumped out the van and tried to kill dat' n****. The van was totaled and I went to jail on New Year's Eve night. Man, I regret it, because it was my fault." The story sounded so familiar. We began asking him question after question. "What color was your mother's van? What did you try to kill the guy with? And what year did it happen, and as he went on to tell the story, it all became clear. What a small world. Gary told Mr. Greens that we were the ones he struck, and we couldn't do anything but fall out in laughter. Who knew we would run into each other again? It was so dark that night and everybody had been drinking except for Carmen and Arielle's girl, whom both were pregnant. There was no way we were going to remember each other's face nearly ten years later.

Another week had gone by and the kids wanted to invite some friends over, so I ordered pizza and we sat around talking, laughing, and playing games. Later that night I had the entire house to myself. Daevon spent the weekend with Diane and Raheem left with the D-family; that was my name for them, because all of their names start with the letter D. Lil' Darnell spent the weekend with his dad and my daughter spent the night with Corina, the little girl who lived in the corner house. Keevon would spend the night with them too, because Corina had two older siblings named Robert and Latosha. Keevon would come home the next day telling me how their mother made him a pie all to himself. It was a blessing to have five children who could all spend the night out at once; I thanked God they weren't bad kids who loved the streets. They definitely weren't menaces to society.

I was up all night as usual, thinking about Keith. I wasn't sick to the stomach as much as before, but I still hadn't gotten over him mentally and emotionally. He so happened to call me as I was lying there looking out the window at the stars. Keith was on the Greyhound headed back to Detroit. He said the relationship hadn't gotten any better, plus he couldn't concentrate on anything because he felt empty without me. Muskegon was boring and too countrified for Keith, so he caused drama in order to make his way back to the "D" by firing gunshots in the air. According to Keith and his boy Derrick, Keith and his family were asked to vacate the premises because of that.

I called Nisha to tell her, but she already knew because he called her first. Nisha was his girl and Stilts was his boy; they had known each other five years before I moved on the block, so I didn't want to take it personal.

I let Keith in through the back door, because of all the gossip that was going on. We stayed up all morning talking about what had been going on with me and up there in Muskegon, and time flew by so quickly. I had to get ready for work. Not too long after I made it to work, Deena came storming in, snatching potato chips off the rack. I assumed her intentions were to see if I had reported to work and that would have perhaps given her a theory as to where Keith was. When she purchased her items and left the store she saw Keith walking up the next block, wondering where he was going and where he spent the night. I'm glad my name didn't come up; I was so lost in love with Keith. Like I said, Keith and Deena's relationship appeared very odd to me, strange. He would cause riffraff just to stay out of her presence, because he knew she would put him out for a few days and he could air out; he didn't want the relationship. I was in a jacked-up situation altogether and couldn't fight the feeling. I hated calling myself a dumb broad, but it seemed to be the case.

Keith and Deena ended up moving back down the street, but that didn't say much about me and his relationship. After moving back Keith became distant. Nisha came by. "What's up with your boy? Deena's acting like she don't want the n**** going nowhere or using the phone, but I'm about to call him." Deena answered the phone and asked Nisha what she wanted. "I need to talk to Keith." She said he was busy so Nisha told her that it was okay, she would see him on the streets. I know that had to piss Deena off. I mean, what man's woman wouldn't be? I didn't say anything. I just sat back and observed. Nisha and Deena were always cool. They were introduced through Keith's cousin Kelsie; she lived with Keith and Deena. Deena, however, didn't care who knew who; she didn't trust anyone around Keith, and I can't say that I blamed her.

Keith's boy Derrick started spending more time at my house; he wanted to persuade me to pray and believe in God only with no Christ in it. To me that was like swimming in an ocean with no arms and legs; bound to drown! But whatever, we started studying the Bible on Saturdays, going back and forth about whether Jesus Christ was just a prophet or the son of the living God. I hadn't found—and truth be told, nor had I thought about finding—a church home since Tennessee. My mind was so lost and all over the place. The only thing I knew to do was to try to survive. I had no dreams, ambitions, didn't know what I was doing with my life or where I was going. I just continued teaching my children what I knew about God in the Bible and training them to remember the books of the bible, different prayers and scriptures by the end of each week. However, long story short, this particular day after Derrick and I were done studying and he left, I kneeled to my knees. "Father, with all due respect I come to you in prayer concerning spiritual truths. Believing that Jesus is your son has always worked for me and has blessed me tremendously. However, I just wanna try something a little different. I need to make sure I'm doing everything right spiritually, even if it means second-guessing myself. I only want to be pleasing in your eyes. I only need one day of having a relationship with you and you only, and praying directly to you without Jesus."

As soon as I said "without Jesus," the Holy Spirit left my body, and at that very moment, it felt like I was living in a world that was just an existence with no leadership or control whatsoever. Immediately I felt empty, with all hope lost. I ended my prayer with "I ask you, Father, to please forgive me right now if I am wrong for not acknowledging Jesus. Amen!" It felt extremely uncomfortable saying "Amen" without saying "in the name of Jesus" first.

That night I had a horrific dream where I was on an airplane from hell. It had been burned in fiery furnace, and was flying so recklessly. The plane then landed and the people sitting across from us, of whom all were women and children began stepping off the plane. There were three limousines parked outside which also had been burned in a fiery furnace; you could tell the plane and limos had come from hell and the pilot was also the driver of the limousines. When my crew began to exit the plane, one of the women from the other group said "oh no, you can't get off the plane yet, you still have more to learn." She shut the door, got in one of the limos and the group left; my group then exited the plane. We walked to a home that seemed to be occupied, but then again it seemed as if it wasn't. I couldn't really determine. We all called for our parents to come get us, because we had no idea where we were. The next morning I fell to my knees. I so needed to get Jesus back on deck. I shamefully asked my father for forgiveness and said, "Please come back, Jesus please!" Immediately I felt the Holy Spirit re-enter inside of me, and I felt whole again. The dream was clearly telling me not to follow Derrick's beliefs. He's the one who lead us on the plane from hell and expected us to follow behind the pilot "aka" devil. I thanked God for not allowing us to follow the group of people to the limo, because they were headed to hell according to how my spirit felt in the dream. Once we exited the plane and ended up at an unknown house to call for our parents was God clearly showing me that: I was becoming a part of the lost souls, which is how we ended up in a foreign land in the first place. Derrick didn't believe Jesus being the son of God. I was considering converting over; thinking I was doing the right thing. The rest of the crew didn't have any God in them at all. We were lost souls in a foreign land, because we didn't know Jesus; we were on the wrong path!

> *There's a one way road to Christ*
> *Don't end up on the other side of the road*
> *Into a head-on collision with the devil.*
> *Joel and Sherese Jordan.*

20

Joel 2:28

I began dreaming one significant dream after another. As usual, it was God's way of communicating with me other than my seeing visions. It was a blessing to know that God hadn't taken his hands off me after all; even if it seemed as though he did, I never gave up on him. I kept praying, because he was all I had. At the end of it all, I knew he was the way out, the truth in my dreams and visions, and he would guide me to the light at the end of the tunnel to new life. I just didn't know when.

The first dream: I was sitting on my front porch talking with my son Keevon when Nisha came walking toward my front porch talking trash. "I'm six months pregnant by Keith and I'm going to have his baby whether you like it or not." All while we were arguing back and forth, my focus was on the tree that stood in my front yard. I completely stopped talking as my focus traveled on the pile of dirt that sat underneath the tree. The pile of dirt had six tree-branch sticks stuck down in it with a star on top of each branch. I eventually turned my back to go into the house as Nisha came trailing right behind me still talking mess, so I told Keevon to watch my back. As I entered the front door, someone was knocking at the back door, so I continued walking in an attempt to see who it was. I cracked the door open just wide enough to see who was on the other side. BAAM! Stilts forced the door open using a humongous, thick, wooden African sculpture and whacked my legs with it three times. I screamed "Holy Ghost!" each time he hit me, because he was so strong that he knocked me off my feet and onto the floor.

Once Nisha saw that Stilts had me down, she reached down in her pocket to pull out a seven-inch dagger with an evil African face sculptured in the handle. Nisha started stabbing the floor in between Keevon's toes, cursing him in a demonic language. I woke up and prayed the 23rd Psalms and continued it in my everyday routine—the dream felt so real and it was so powerful that it distilled fear in my heart. I thought about when Stilts used to talk about how his family casted witchcraft on his mother and it killed her. I don't know how true it was, but I was aware of the Bible speaking on such evil in Galatians 5:19-21.

From the time I had that dream, things began to take a turn for the worse. I began having dreams of losing one of my children. Nisha portrayed to be a cool chick, but my spirit only allowed me to deal with her in a cordial manner. I remember when she wanted to style Diane's hair, but my spirit said no so I left it that way, and it was all because of the dream.

A couple weeks later the kids on the block were gossiping about Nisha's ultrasound photos. From that day forward every time Keith pulled into my driveway he had Usher Raymond's "Confession" song on blast; it was his way of telling me...he'd messed up! Knowing Keith wasn't my man, I was still devastated because I was in love. Other than Nisha playing me like she did, I couldn't get that upset with her either, because she and I both were messing around with someone else's man. Unfortunately, I had no idea. I mean, I never looked that deep into Keith and Nisha's friendship, because they were already friends' years before me. If Deena didn't look into it, I didn't feel I needed to either, especially if I hadn't heard any rumors, but that was the kids on the block starting gossip, and by then it was all too late. The difference between Nisha and I was I wasn't pretending to be Deena's friend. She was down-right scandalous. I then understood the dream of me swimming with the fish; I was in association with the chick that was pregnant by the guy I was in love with.

The second dream: Deena was talking with a friend of hers and he was telling her that he was in love with her. She turned her back, faced the guy, and said, "Vice versa, but I don't want any trouble out of Keith." When I looked at the back of her shirt there were four numbers written in yellow marker: 3777. I woke up. That number played for fish and trouble; I played the number in the lottery, both the three and four digits. I just knocked off one of the sevens when I played the three digits. Both Deena and I dreamed about fish within days of each other. I dreamt I was swimming with the fish; I told my daughter Dejah, who thought it was hilarious. Of course I didn't think it was so funny. I wondered if Deena was swimming with the fish in her dream too.

Deep down, Keith had a gut feeling Nisha's baby wasn't his, but he knew he laid up with her just as other guys had, so there was a possibility of him being the father. He started sneaking over to Nisha's at night in an effort not to get caught, but all was too late; Nisha's pregnancy could only be kept quiet for so long. As much as I loved that song "Confession," I hated it all the more, because that song had become my reality. Keith couldn't apologize enough. I was so deeply wounded...again. And still...I was in love with that boy!

I hit both numbers within days of each other. I hit 377 for five hundred and 3777 for little over a thousand. I had no idea how Keith knew I hit the lottery, besides my young, mouthy boss who kicked it with everybody in the hood. Keith met up with me on the way home from the store, but Jesus had my focus on the church members as they were all approaching their vehicles after service. There was a man dressed in a white suit accented in purple. Jesus told me to give my tithes to him and so I did. Keith started laughing at me. "You just gave away fifty dollars to a man you don't even know." Once we were half way up the block, the man yelled out to me "What's your name so I write on the can envelope?" I gave him my name. I told Keith I was led to give my tithes to that man specifically, and whether he paid my tithes or pocketed the money, God was surely going to bless me. Watch God bless me! I surely wasn't gonna give it to Keith. Keith stopped laughing then, because he knew every time I told him something God said or did, it always came to pass.

The third dream: Dejah and I were in the ocean, and she was on a raft as I was floating in the water next to her. A whirlpool spun me around, pulling me in the opposite direction from my daughter. I tried so hard to keep focused on her, but the wind started blowing her in the opposite direction from me. She reached out for me, screaming, "Mommy, help me!" but every time I tried to swim toward her, the whirlpool twirled me farther back in the opposite direction. The wind continued pulling my daughter away from me; I woke up.

The fourth dream: I was preparing seafood shish kebobs to be cooked on the grill. I layered small fish on a stick one by one. After I woke up, I called Nina's grandmother and told her about the dream. She said, "Honey, that sounds like child death to me." It didn't matter how in depth my prayers were or how often I prayed, the dreams became more and more intense.

The fifth dream: I was walking home from the store and as I turned onto my block, there I saw Keevon being attacked by a black crow underneath the same tree that was in my previous dream about Nisha. I stopped in my tracks; after the crow attacked my son, I saw a flock of them attacking the rest of the kids who were playing up and down the street. Children were screaming and running everywhere.

I woke up and stepped outside on my front porch while the block was still sound asleep. I looked to God. "Father, I keep having these dreams of losing one of my children. If you're trying to test me to see if I will turn my back on you, I won't. When you removed me from the domestic violence relationship with Gino, I told you I would never turn my back on you, and I meant that. But if it is your will to bring one of us home, let your will be done!" I went back into the house and let it be—not to say that I didn't worry because I did; I was only being human. These dreams were clearly telling me that great destruction was bound to happen. A destruction so great that it would totally be out of my control, as if it had to come to pass.

My life and everything around it had begun to spin out of control even more. I couldn't go to work without coming home and finding my back door wide open, because some kids had been in and out doing God knows what. My sons seemed to be dumb to the fact, because they couldn't give me any answers and I was surprised at them. I've always had my sons pretty much under control. In an attempt to diminish the situation, I decided to quit my job and prepared myself to move immediately and with no money; it was time to go. Everybody was nosy and trying to be all in my business, because like I said, it seemed as if Keith and I were the celeb couple in the hood. I had completely lost control over my life. I was traumatically worn down. Nisha started walking on the other side of the street, afraid that I was going to break her in half. As much as I wanted to kill Keith first and foremost, and then Nisha, I could never put my hands on a pregnant woman. It wasn't my place to do that anyway, because at the end of the day, Keith was neither my man nor Nisha's to be fighting over. Keith and Nisha were so scandalous. They were sexing before he left for Muskegon. I reminisced about the time when Nisha and Stilts came by the house to so-call comfort me when Keith first left. I was lying on a snake while getting bit on the back of my neck. Nisha was hanging at Deena and Keith's house when Deena was at work. Nisha was laughing in Deena's face while spitting out venom on me to make her look good. Deena was rubbing Nisha's belly, talking to the baby, not having a freakin' clue that she was caressing her own stepchild. People tried telling Deena about the baby, but her mind was too stuck on me. People on the block would ask me, "Have you seen Deena today? She dyed her hair and styled it just like yours; she even wears the same style sunglasses you wear, trying to look like you!"

The sixth dream: The kids and I were moving out of the house. We grabbed our luggage and walked toward the front door, and there was a large crack in the floor from one corner of my baseboard, all the way to the end of the wall. All you could see was a large trail of black dirt along the baseboard and demonic arms reaching up, trying to pull me down. Their arms looked as if they were burned in a furnace; they were black and ashy and had fingernails like gargoyles. Out of nowhere they snatched me down and I screamed out "Jesus!" three times. I was looking at my children while trying to muster up enough strength to get back up on my feet. Before I could blink my eyes I was lifted up powerfully in midair and back on my feet. The demons were still reaching for me as we all walked away from the house without ever looking back.

My world was continuously spinning out of control. Keith was worn down from Nisha, feeling guilty about the pregnancy and how he played Deena…and me. He was ready to move off the block away from all the drama that he caused. As for me, I was still in love. I couldn't let go. I didn't know what the heck was happening to me besides just being plain stupid. Keith was stressed out, wanting to get away just like me, but again, he caused it all. I hadn't mentioned anything about moving, not even to the kids. I didn't want anybody in my business anymore than they already were. I just needed to get away. I definitely wasn't going to tell the kids, especially since I didn't know who was running in and out of our house trashing it. Who knows? Deena or Nisha may have had something to do with it. I mean after all, Deena hated me, and Nisha was obviously jealous of me. She had years to fool around with Keith, but, when he and I became hot topics in the hood, all of a sudden she wanted a piece of the limelight - in the HOOD! I was never a hood chick, even Keith knew that.

Keith was apologetic for all he had done to me, and wanted to move away so we could start fresh; he didn't want to lose me. I heard from a number of people, including Keith, that Nisha was hanging out with Kelsie and her man and they got stoned off ecstasy pills. Nisha claimed Kelsie and her man slipped a mickey in her drink and sexually seduced her. Allegedly Nisha woke up the next morning in their bed naked, and this was right around the time she got pregnant. However, that situation still didn't justify the fact that Keith screwed Nisha and very well may be the father of that child.

Unfortunately, I sent the older boys with Diane until I

could find another house, plus she was very ill and I knew she could use some support.

If it wasn't one thing, it was another, and all of it didn't just have to do with Keith and me. There was so much tension and drama going on throughout family homes up and down the street, as if the entire block was cursed and sat on top of a gravesite or something. Everybody on the block was fighting everybody all the time and I had more haters than I ever had in my life. This was a first to have as many enemies as I did, especially all at once, and I believe Keith was the foundation of it all. It had nothing to do with me messing around with him while he was with Deena, because no one liked her, period. For some reason or another, everybody was just drawn to be in the mix of Keith and me. I understood Deena's anger with me, but Nisha was a snake.

The other lady who I felt didn't care too much for me was Latosha's mother; her name was Latosha too. We talked cordially with one another concerning our children, especially if they were spending nights back and forth together, but that was it. I thought maybe she didn't like me, because of my relationship with her daughter, because their relationship was rocky. Latosha used to come down to the house sobbing about the things her mother had done or said to her and how she was an alcoholic. The only sincere and common thing I knew to do was be an ear to her and from there, direct her straight to the Bible. I tried mending their relationship by explaining why parents sometimes say the things they say and do the things they do, that at the end of the day…it was all love. I spent a lot of time with all of the children on the block talking to them about God. I used to grill hamburgers and hot dogs or order pizza just to spend some quality time with them. It was another way of keeping up with the type of kids my children were hanging out with.

The seventh dream: I was at Diane's house, sitting in the family room, and I looked down through the floor and saw five dolphins in water looking up at me, trying to tell me something. A lady sitting next to me was showing me how to communicate with the dolphins by placing a signature whistle to my ear. I was focused on the fifth dolphin, because it was the only one not communicating, only flipping in and out of the water. That's what Lil' Darnell did all day every day when he wasn't hooping; no hand backward flips. Those five dolphins represented my children. As I was watching the dolphin on the end do flips, I was listening to the dolphin sounds through the signature whistle. Whatever the dolphins were saying to me brought on the most unbearable, excruciating labor pains I had ever felt in my entire life.

I bore five children, two of whom were identical twins. The labor pains I felt in reality giving birth to them were nowhere near what I had experienced in this dream.

The last dream: I was standing outside, looking across the sky as five white doves flew across in an arrow shape. I looked down and saw a white stone imbedded with diamonds and crystals; I picked it up and threw it at the doves. As I watched the stone shoot across the sky, I started thinking, *why am I throwing a stone at the doves? I don't want to hurt them.* The stone struck one of the dove's wings but it didn't flinch; they were flying strong.

I woke up. The number 1112 played for birds and babies in the lottery. I longed for a sweet dream after so many negative ones. I actually took this dream to be a blessing because of the white doves. I gave the number to Diane and a friend of mine; she was going through financial difficulties just like me. I had five dollars to my name, so I wheeled the number and boxed it then gave the boxed ticket to Diane.

I hit the lottery for five thousand dollars. I guess each dove was worth a thousand dollars; Diane and my friend were so grateful. I paid down on what I called my new mean-green Lincoln machine and off I went shopping for all my children. I gave my older sons a few hundred dollars. I went back to the neighborhood to retrieve some things from the old house. I gave all the kids on the block five dollars each and fifty dollars to Keevon's very best friends, Robert Jr. and Raymond. I paid my tithes again to a church my neighbors attended, but knew them very well, entrusting them to do the right thing and they did. I told Keith *"I told you God was going to bless me"*.

> *The Lord won't bless you in no mess,*
> *but He'll surely Bless your way out of it.*
> *Sherese L. Jordan*

21

The Signs

The first sign: I informed my caseworker that I was moving, so she mailed all the paperwork I needed to fill out. Everything I needed was in the yellow package, including a burial funding application. I immediately balled it up and threw it in the trash. However, my spirit strongly encouraged me to keep it for future use, but I didn't because I wasn't trying to claim it. I tried ignoring the fact that I ever laid eyes on it.

The second sign: Deena came home from work and told Keith a prophet walked up to her at work and said, "When you're here at work, women are hanging out at your house and your son's father is unfaithful to you. He is suppose to die in the house down the street, but God has something else in store for him. God is going to take away all of your pain and give it to your son's father, and he is going to feel it for the rest of his life."

I don't know if Keith told Deena he was leaving her again for me or what happened. I only remember Keith coming to my house with a garbage bag filled with clothes and shoes, and when he dumped everything out, they were all in shreds. Deena had moved back to Muskegon. He was so upset, not understanding why Deena couldn't just love him enough to let him go but let him continue to be a father to his son. But again, according to him her words were always "If you leave me, you leave family!"

Keith and Diane had a good relationship, which wasn't surprising, because they were pretty much cut from the same cloth. Whenever Diane needed to get somebody's hands dirty, Keith, Gary, and a few other guys in the hood were the ones to do the job.

Diane let Keith move in with her until we found a new home. Again, he was wanting to get away from Deena and everybody else who was in our business. Although Diane didn't want me living with her, a week later I tagged right behind the rest of the fam. My children had already been there for a few days, and they were my responsibility. I felt like if Keith could stay there why couldn't I? I knew the kids being there wouldn't last for long, because Diane didn't have that same grandmotherly love for them as she did for Daevon, and she especially didn't care too much for my daughter, but I'm sure she loved her. She loved them all, but Daevon was her pride and joy.

Once we were all settled at Diane's for about a week, I lucked up on a job. I also laid down some ground rules concerning company, especially since Diane's health wasn't in the best condition. I was working afternoons and I needed the boys to help be responsible for themselves, and for their younger siblings. I also needed them to respect Diane's house, considering she already didn't want us there; only Daevon, Gary, and Keith. I surely wasn't trying to turn her house into a flop. I was tired of that myself after dang near raising thirteen kids: my kids, Carmen's kids, Arielle's kids, and then some. I remember

Darnell coming by to visit one day, and when he walked through the door he said, "My house is cleaner than yours and I live on the streets!" Carmen thought that was hilarious and she laughed herself sick! I, on the other hand, didn't find it hilarious at all. That was just another sign that my life had spiraled out of control.

21

The Havoc

Deena called looking for Keith. She seemed anxious as if it was an emergency. According to Keith some guys had kicked in the front door looking for her sister, but she wasn't home. They made Deena and her two sons lie face-down on the floor at gunpoint because her sister owed them money. The guys didn't hurt them, they just wanted word to spread; thank God! I told Keith to go get his family and bring them back to the city. At that point I had to put my emotions aside and do what was right in my heart, especially with children being involved. I stayed home so I could get my kids situated and myself ready for work. I didn't know whether to trust Keith or not as far as trying to hook back up with Deena, but I wasn't concerned about that; my only concern was getting her and those kids back to safety.

Keith bought a new video game for the boys. We couldn't keep things like that at the old house, because kids were stealing and trashing my house. Keith and I made sure the boys had a clear understanding about company not coming over to the house.

That whole "ground rule laying thing" went through one ear and out the other. Robert and Raymond came by to visit while Keith and I were out. When we came home everybody was trying to explain how the video game came up missing all at one time; it disappeared when Robert and Raymond left.

The next morning Keith and I went to the old neighborhood, which was something we did every day to retrieve my mail from the old house. Afterward we went by Robert and Latosha's house to inquire about the game. Robert thought everything was funny as usual, claiming he didn't take it. I knew he was lying, because he played so many games and thought everything was funny. Before we moved off the block, he used to stick his head through my front window acting silly. I had to tell him time and time again to stop. His mama let him do whatever he wanted to as far as I was concerned, because she was an ignorant and ghetto chick from what I'd heard from a number of sources, which is probably why we didn't click.

Keith had gotten frustrated altogether, not only because of Robert's insincerity, but Latosha's nasty, sassy mouth. Latosha had previously changed her attitude toward me because I wouldn't take her to visit her boyfriend Jessie, who'd recently gotten locked up. I took her once, but then after that I had to take thought in what I was doing. What if I had a sixteen-year-old daughter and some grown woman was taking her to a prison to visit a twenty-two-year-old thug that I disapproved of and didn't know much about? I would be highly upset! So at the end of the day, I believe that's what changed how Latosha felt about me.

Words were exchanged and during all the commotion Robert and I were the only two talking civilly. I buried the hatchet right then and thought, "it was cool; our loss"! I hated that I had to accept that. People just do whatever they want all because the court system is so jacked up in Detroit, it's pathetic. It takes forever to receive what's owed to a person after winning a case and that's if the defendant feels like paying. If not, you have to file a suit all over again; basically you're just wasting your time and money on court fees, because in most small claim courts it's likely you wont receive a dime.

Keith couldn't leave well enough alone; he blacked out. He started throwing rocks at their front window and I grabbed him, yelling, "It's not that serious. We'll just buy another game!" But the game wasn't the problem; it was Robert's insincerity and Latosha's threats that rubbed Keith the wrong way. I couldn't calm Keith down. The more I screamed, the madder he got and started smashing the windows with his bare hands. He wasn't trying to hurt anyone physically, because if he was, he could have easily done so; everyone was outside. In his mind, breaking the windows was some sort of replacement of the game. Robert was so irritating, he played too much all the time. Latosha on the other hand, had then grown angrier, cursing up a storm as I finally got Keith away and we left. I was heated with Keith because he took things way out of context. The only thing that ran through my head was "Someone could've gotten hurt". Keith drove to a friend's house, but I went straight home, because deep down in my spirit something didn't feel right.

Passing back through the neighborhood after dropping Keith off, I heard sirens. I wanted to ride back by Latosha's to make sure everything was okay, but after Keith went ballistic I knew that the family was angry at that point. They were probably thinking I brought Keith over there to start trouble, but that wasn't my intention. My only intention was to resolve the situation in a peaceful manner. Latosha's mother already didn't care for me too much in the first place, and I never knew why, so it definitely wouldn't have been wise to go back over there, and especially alone. My focus was going straight home. I had a feeling the police were on the way. I needed to step up to the plate since I was the one who took Keith over there. Although I was trying to be the peacemaker in the midst of all of the chaos, I was guilty, because I was an accessory to the crime. I had no idea Keith would flip the script that way and cause something so detrimental.

I was incarcerated and my car was towed away of course, being it was involved in the crime. Latosha's youngest sister Corina was hit in the head with one of the stones and needed stitches. I tossed and turned all night in my cell, praying to God for peace, because apparently I didn't have enough power to put the situation at ease. If I hadn't inquired about the game and just said forget it, none of what happened would have ever taken place. But I had allowed people to run over me so much that I was tired of that, and although Keith stood up for what was right, he went about it the wrong way. I knew he wasn't physically trying to hurt anybody, but he lost his temper instead of thinking first. He didn't take into consideration that throwing stones at somebody's window could result in someone potentially getting hurt. You never know whose on the other side. I had so many thoughts trampling through my head that it was overwhelming.

I was released the next day without being charged. Keith, however, was a different story. The cops were definitely after him.

Diane picked me up from the precinct. On the way home we stopped at the nearest store because I was in need of a cigarette, bad. As we were driving I saw Robert and Latosha's mother following closely behind us; when we found a nearby store we pulled over and parked. As soon as I stepped out of the van, Latosha, her mother, and her friend jumped me. Diane struggled to get in between me and them, as they swung at me trying to maneuver so they wouldn't hit her. At that point I had no choice but to swing back. They were beyond angry and at that point talking was not an option.

Keith and Darnell were at the house when we arrived. We told them what happened. Keith knew the police were after him, and he wasn't trying to hide; he felt like it was all bound to come to a head. When all was said and done, Keith felt extremely bad; he had no intentions of anyone getting hurt physically. Although I was trying to keep the peace during the commotion when it all first started, I have to say that I wasn't upset for how they reacted toward me. The average family would've reacted the same way. Latosha and Robert saw that I was dealing with the situation in a respectful manner from the very beginning, even to the point where I was trying to calm Keith down. But like I said Latosha felt bitter towards me after I decided it wasn't a good idea taking her to visit a man in jail and an older man at that. Plus her mother didn't too much care for me like I'd mentioned before, so for that reason, that gave them the urge to act out the way that they did. I sat around all weekend feeling devastated about everything that had taken place.

Monday was gray and gloomy. I woke up feeling tranquilized after mourning all weekend long. The chaos wasn't over… it was only the beginning! I could feel it deep down in my soul. Monday felt extremely weird. I kept my kids home from school. Lil' Darnell and Dejah attended the elementary school in the old neighborhood, and on the way home from school, they would have to pass by Robert and Latosha's house. This particular day something told me to leave them at home. It was evident that Latosha and her family were extremely furious with me and I didn't want to take any chances.

I kept to myself at work because the thought of all that had taken place over the weekend was still overwhelming. Before long, I looked up and saw everyone focusing on the police as they made their way straight to me. I was needed at home. At this time, I felt more tranquilized than I did over the past weekend. The spirit was holding me so tight that I almost felt as if I couldn't move; I knew something was wrong because I was too relaxed. My coworker Meechie had been telling me for almost a month about a bad feeling he kept having.

I was quiet the entire ride. Once I turned onto my block, I saw that my street was flooded with people, and red, white, and blue lights lit the sky up like it was the fourth of July. FOX 2 News was on the scene and the Channel 4 news helicopter was circling the surrounding area. We had to park all the way at the end of the block, because down by my end it was closed off with yellow tape; Lord God! I jumped out of the car, leaving Meechie behind, trying to run through the yellow tape. The entire block instantaneously went silent and the cops embraced me firmly. I never experienced such a silent moment in all my days of living. My body was calm, from my spirit to my soul and through my mind. I was in silent mode. I couldn't think. I was blank. God only allowed me to hear whispering among the cops, but a vision streamed across my eyes just before the whispering started. It was a news clip I'd saw years ago about a lady who was standing in the middle of the street, just like I was at that very moment. The cops had her embraced as they gave her the bad news. She then fell back on the pavement spinning around in circles using her feet as she screamed and cried out beyond any pain imaginable.

Here I was living in the crisis of her reality. I went into a trance. I had no control. Everything started to stream in slow motion just as it did when I was in the bad car accident. Once the vision disappeared, I then heard what the cop said to the other cop; everything continued to take place in slow motion. I fell back flat onto the pavement in the middle of the street as my eyes gazed into the sky. Instantly it started raining on my face as if...the angels were crying! I screamed beyond any pain imaginable! At that very moment I felt that unbearable labor pain that I'd felt in my dream. I would've never thought, that beyond that yellow tape, was one of my very own.......

Epilogue Part II

I was sitting on the porch and the mailman was walking down the street delivering mail. He stopped when he approached my house like he normally did and spoke. The only difference was this time he had worry in his eyes. "Good morning. How are you today?" He asked as he was handing me my mail. "I'm doing okay. How about yourself?" I responded. "I'm hanging in there. Did you hear about the situation that had taken place not too far from here?" "No, what happened?" I asked in a curious tone. "Someone was shot and..." "OH MY GOD!" Was it fatal?" I asked cutting him short as paranoia began to take over me and my chest began to feel heavy with grief. "Yes. Someone was shot in the head."

At that precise moment I fell to my knees in great agony crying beyond distress with my head buried in the palm of my hands. The pain in my chest was unbearable.

I jolted awake with tears in my eyes. It was just a dream, but knowing my dreams tend to have significant meanings I fell to my knees and began to praise God, I prayed and I begged God for protection, but the dream only became more and more intense; informative and reoccurring.

I continued to dream this same nightmare every-so-often as a sign that, this too must come to pass....

About the Author

Sherese L. Jordan is a servant of Jesus the Christ. She is a wife, mother, and grandmother. Sherese is an author and composer of multiple written poetical and fictional works. Sherese is also very creative. She has her own business where she custom designs floor model lamps (diormahogany.com). She enjoys reading, exercising, and traveling, and she is an excellent cook. As a survivor of various traumatic incidents, Sherese was inspired by God to share her testimony. Her goal is to be an inspiration to the children of God, in telling her testimony of how the Lord brought her through everything that happened in her life of which all, was in divine order. Always remember: when the devil continuously attacks you, it's because the anointing is on you; you're spiritually powerful. You belong to the most high God. God is going to use you and the devil hates that, that's why he throws stumbling blocks in your pathway to keep you from carrying out God's Will. "Your passion is your talent. Your talent is your calling. Your calling is what brings God the glory!

Printed in the USA
CPSIA information can be obtained
at www.ICGtesting.com
JSHW081908191123
52095JS00001B/68